Written by

Trisha Callella

Editor: Alaska Hults
Illustrator: Corbin Hillam
Cover Illustrator: Rick Grayson
Designer: Moonhee Pak
Cover Designer: Moonhee Pak
Art Director: Tom Cochrane
Project Director: Carolea Williams

Table of Contents

Introduction

Mathematical Thinking focuses on six math standards that students rarely experience in a multiple-choice, timed-testing format. For example, students often build patterns with connecting cubes (or similar toys such as LEGO®s), but they often fail to understand how to identify in a multiple-choice format the answer that shows a missing element in a pattern. The problems in *Mathematical Thinking* give students the opportunity to practice specific math concepts in a multiple-choice format.

Mathematical Thinking contains in a standardized-test format 15 problem sets (a page of three problems) for each math standard. The first page of each *Mathematical Thinking* section provides a brief definition of the targeted concept, one or two ideas for supporting that concept in an interactive way, and test-taking tips that students can use to improve their performance on multiple-choice tests. The second page of each section is a chart that cross-references the specific math concepts that students need to solve each problem set. An answer key is provided at the end of each section.

Each problem set has three levels of difficulty. The ⬤ problem introduces the concept, the ▲ problem provides an opportunity to independently practice the concept, and the ⬛ problem provides a more challenging application of the concept. Each problem has an Extend the Thinking question that encourages students to either build on the information in the problem or to communicate their reasoning. Because the purpose of the problems is to help students build test-taking skills and to provide practice with the math standards, it is helpful to do the problem sets in a whole-class setting. Refer to How to Use This Book (page 4) to decide how to implement the problem sets in a way that fits your teaching style and math curriculum.

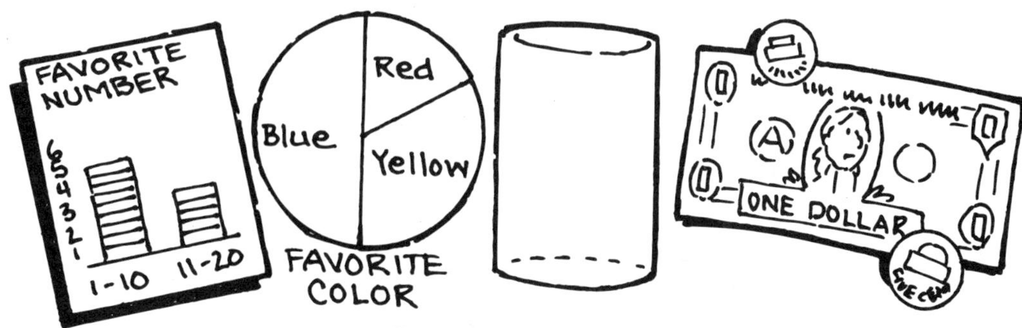

How to Use This Book

Choose a problem set, and photocopy it for each student. Make an overhead transparency of the problem set to facilitate class discussion. Read aloud the first problem, and discuss it as a class. Demonstrate how to fill in the answer bubbles, and then have students work together (in pairs or small groups) on the ● problem. Be sure to have them complete on the back of their paper the Extend the Thinking problem. Then, refer to the answer page at the end of each section, and discuss the solution as a class. Invite students to share how they solved the problem as well as the actual solution. Then, either assign both the ▲ and ■ problems for students to work on individually, or have each student solve a developmentally appropriate problem (steering more fluent math students toward the ■ problem). After students have completed their work, discuss both problems as a class.

Keep in mind that the purpose of the problem sets is to teach students how to solve problems in a multiple-choice format. If the class seems to be struggling with a specific concept, set aside the problems, teach the concept in your usual math instruction, and then return to the problems when students are ready.

Present problem sets within each section sequentially. You may choose to have students complete a given section or one problem set from each section (to cover up to five concepts in one week). At the start of each week, introduce one test-taking strategy (from the first page of each section), and encourage students to practice that strategy during the week. Focus on a general tip, such as getting necessary rest the night before a test, or on specific concepts, such as how to solve analogy problems.

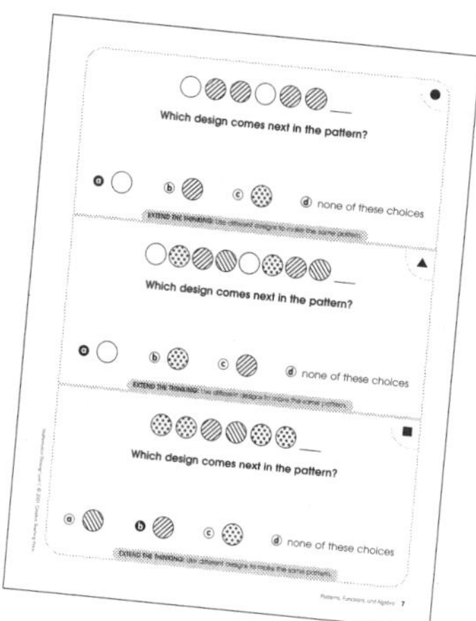

Patterns, Functions, and Algebra

The *Level D* Patterns, Functions, and Algebra standards require students to

- extend symbolic or numeric patterns

- identify a missing element in a pattern

- apply the concept of a pattern to a real-life situation

- identify number patterns that occur in real life

Pattern Pairs

Divide the class into pairs. Give one student in each pair a plastic bag filled with connecting blocks (e.g., LEGO®'s, Mega Bloks® by Ritvik Toys®). Ask that student to use the blocks to make a pattern. When the student is finished, have the partner extend the pattern. Have partners switch roles so each student has a chance to make a pattern and extend a pattern.

Class Store

Set up a class "store." Write on a large piece of chart paper the items for "sale" and their prices. List individual items and different groups of items. Have students calculate which items or groups of items would be the best value.

Concepts: Patterns, Functions, and Algebra

Math Concept	Problem Set	page 7	page 8	page 9	page 10	page 11	page 12	page 13	page 14	page 15	page 16	page 17	page 18	page 19	page 20	page 21
Patterns		X	X	X	X	X	X			X	X	X				
Functions								X	X				X	X		
Algebra															X	X
Shapes						X							X			
Addition/Subtraction Multiplication/Division			X	X		X	X			X	X	X		X	X	X
Tables										X	X	X				

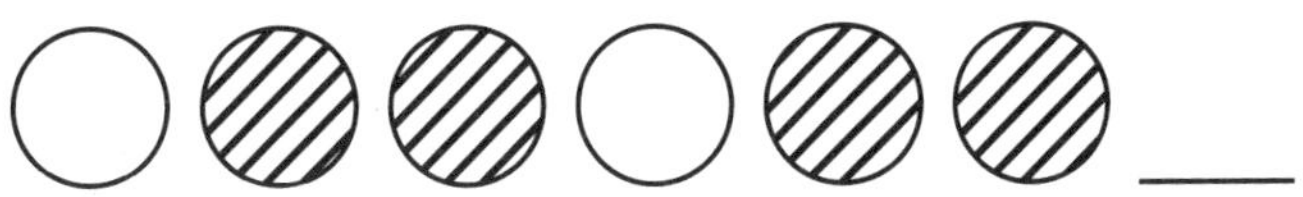

Which design comes next in the pattern?

 **a**    **b**   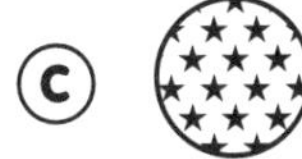 **c**   **d** none of these choices

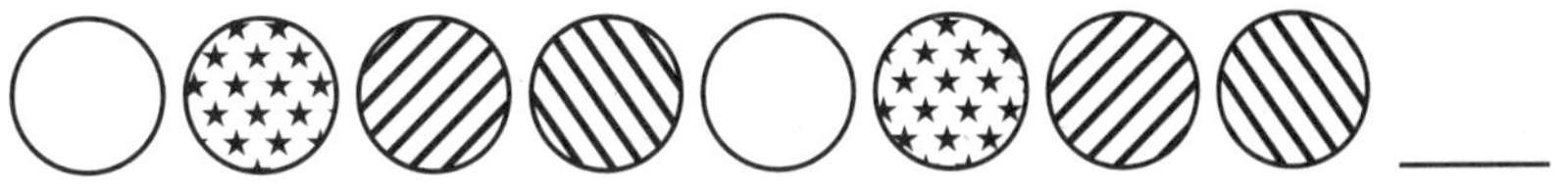

Which design comes next in the pattern?

 **a**    **b**   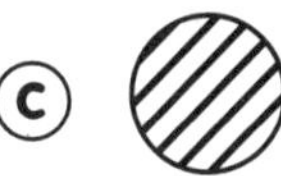 **c**   **d** none of these choices

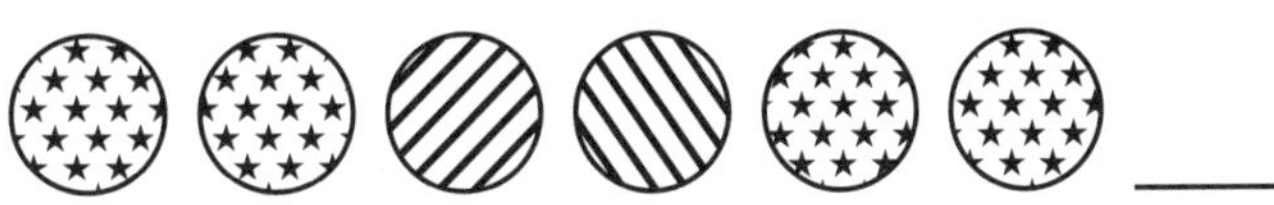

Which design comes next in the pattern?

a    **b**    **c**    **d** none of these choices

Which design comes next in the pattern?

 ⓐ    ⓑ    ⓒ   ⓓ none of these choices

EXTEND THE THINKING: Use different designs to make the same pattern.

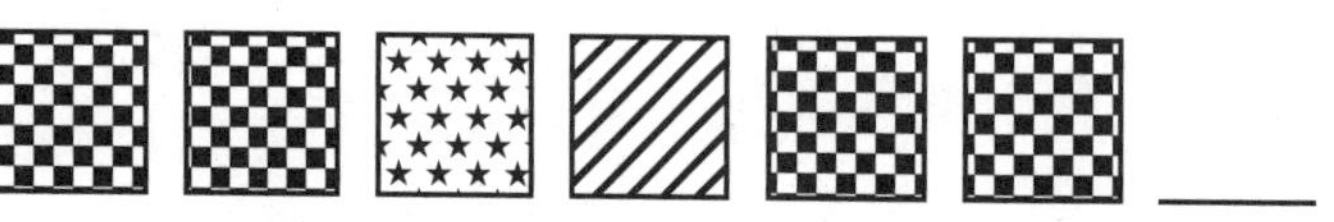

Which design comes next in the pattern?

ⓐ    ⓑ    ⓒ 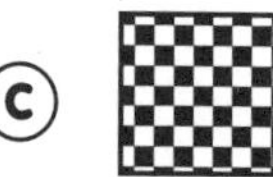   ⓓ none of these choices

EXTEND THE THINKING: Use different designs to make the same pattern.

Which design comes next in the pattern?

ⓐ    ⓑ    ⓒ    ⓓ none of these choices

EXTEND THE THINKING: Describe the pattern.

7 6 5 4 3 ____

Which number comes next in the pattern?

(a) 1   (b) 2   (c) 0   (d) 4

EXTEND THE THINKING: Describe the pattern.

---

50 40 30 20 ____

Which number comes next in the pattern?

(a) 10   (b) 0   (c) 15   (d) 30

EXTEND THE THINKING: Describe the pattern.

---

16 8 4 2 ____

Which number comes next in the pattern?

(a) 15   (b) 1   (c) 0   (d) 12

EXTEND THE THINKING: Describe the pattern.

15   14   13   12   ____

Which number comes next in the pattern?

   (a) 10   (b) 11   (c) 9   (d) 13

EXTEND THE THINKING: Describe the pattern.

9   7   5   3   ____

Which number comes next in the pattern?

   (a) 0   (b) 2   (c) 4   (d) 1

EXTEND THE THINKING: Describe the pattern.

56   28   14   ____

Which number comes next in the pattern?

   (a) 7   (b) 10   (c) 13   (d) 1

EXTEND THE THINKING: Describe the pattern.

Which shape is missing in the pattern?

a   b   c   d

Which shape is missing in the pattern?

a   b   c   d

Which shape is missing in the pattern?

a   b   c   d

5   7   ____   11   13   15

Which number is missing in the pattern?

(a) 12   (b) 14   (c) 9   (d) 8

4   7   ____   13   16   19

Which number is missing in the pattern?

(a) 9   (b) 10   (c) 13   (d) 6

4   9   ____   19   24   29

Which number is missing in the pattern?

(a) 14   (b) 10   (c) 17   (d) 15

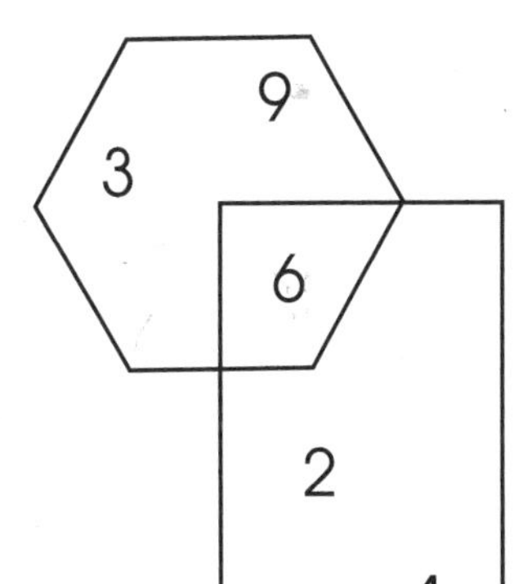

Which number is only in the hexagon?

(a) 7 (b) 9 (c) 4 (d) 2

EXTEND THE THINKING: Explain how you solved the problem.

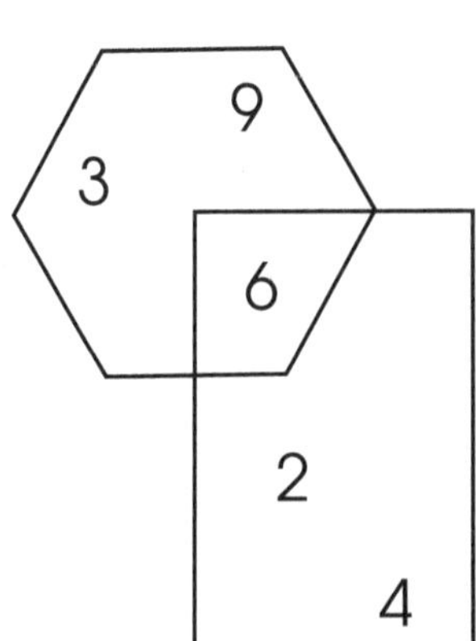

Which number is in the rectangle and the hexagon?

(a) 7 (b) 9 (c) 6 (d) 2

EXTEND THE THINKING: Explain how you solved the problem.

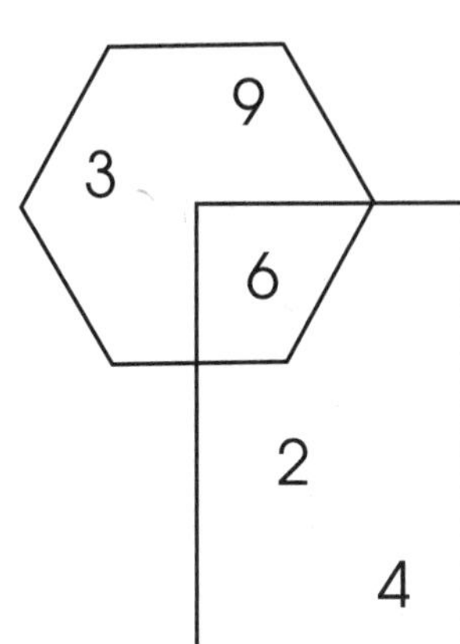

Which number could go in the hexagon but not in the rectangle?

(a) 12 (b) 15 (c) 16 (d) 22

EXTEND THE THINKING: Explain how you solved the problem.

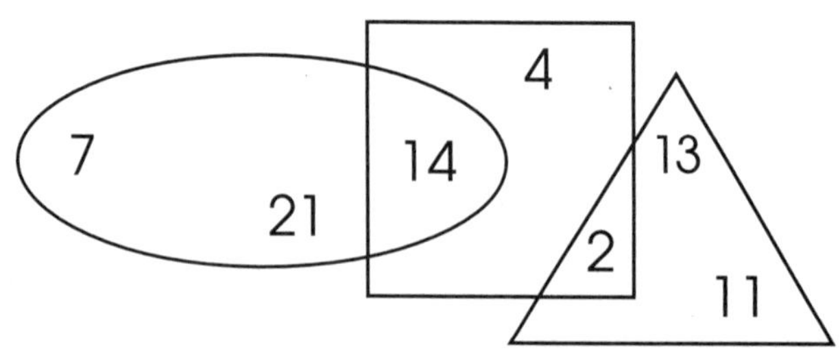

Which number is only in the square?

(a) 4 (b) 6 (c) 14 (d) 2

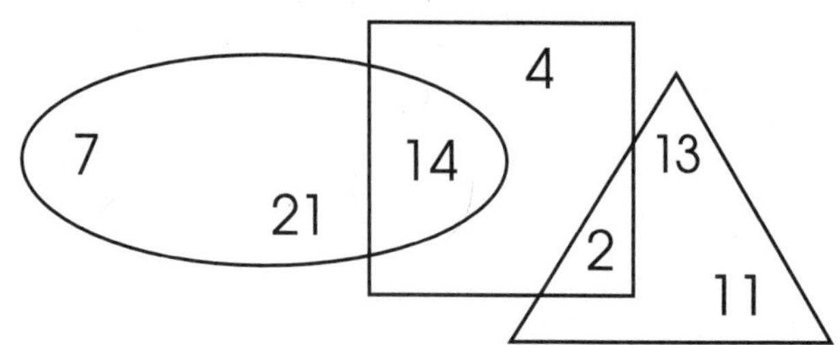

Which number could also go in the square?

(a) 3 (b) 8 (c) 11 (d) 9

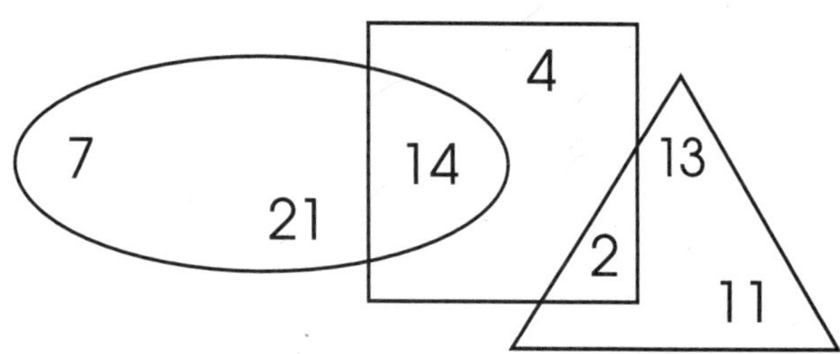

Which number could go in the oval but not in the square?

(a) 35 (b) 28 (c) 42 (d) 56

Jelly Beans Eaten

Monday	Tuesday	Wednesday
1	3	5

How many jelly beans were eaten on Thursday if the pattern continued?

ⓐ 1   **ⓑ** 7   **ⓒ** 30   **ⓓ** none of these choices

EXTEND THE THINKING: Describe the pattern.

Jelly Beans Eaten

Monday	Tuesday	Wednesday
1	4	7

How many jelly beans were eaten on Thursday if the pattern continued?

ⓐ 1   **ⓑ** 10   **ⓒ** 30   **ⓓ** none of these choices

EXTEND THE THINKING: Describe the pattern.

Jelly Beans Eaten

Monday	Tuesday	Wednesday
1	5	9

How many jelly beans were eaten on Thursday if the pattern continued?

ⓐ 1   **ⓑ** 13   **ⓒ** 30   **ⓓ** none of these choices

EXTEND THE THINKING: Describe the pattern.

Fish Bought

Tuesday	Wednesday	Thursday
1	2	3

How many fish were bought on Friday if the pattern continued?

(a) 50   (b) 1   (c) 0   (d) none of these choices

EXTEND THE THINKING: Describe the pattern.

Fish Bought

Tuesday	Wednesday	Thursday
3	5	7

How many fish were bought on Friday if the pattern continued?

(a) 9   (b) 1   (c) 12   (d) none of these choices

EXTEND THE THINKING: Describe the pattern.

Fish Bought

Tuesday	Wednesday	Thursday
4	8	12

How many fish were bought on Friday if the pattern continued?

(a) 16   (b) 24   (c) 9   (d) none of these choices

EXTEND THE THINKING: Describe the pattern.

Points Earned in Basketball

game 1	game 2	game 3
2	4	6

How many points were earned in game 4 if the pattern continued?

ⓐ 8 **ⓑ** 12 **ⓒ** 1 **ⓓ** none of these choices

EXTEND THE THINKING: Use shapes to make the same pattern.

Points Earned in Basketball

game 1	game 2	game 3
3	5	7

How many points were earned in game 4 if the pattern continued?

ⓐ 5 **ⓑ** 9 **ⓒ** 15 **ⓓ** none of these choices

EXTEND THE THINKING: Use shapes to make the same pattern.

Points Earned in Basketball

game 1	game 2	game 3
4	7	10

How many points were earned in game 4 if the pattern continued?

ⓐ 13 **ⓑ** 12 **ⓒ** 21 **ⓓ** none of these choices

EXTEND THE THINKING: Use shapes to make the same pattern.

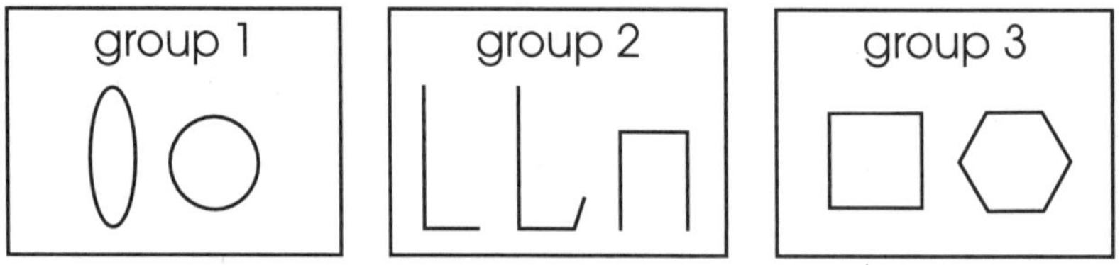

group 1 group 2 group 3

In which group does ⬯ belong?

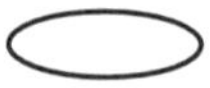

a group 1   **b** group 2   **c** group 3   **d** none of these choices

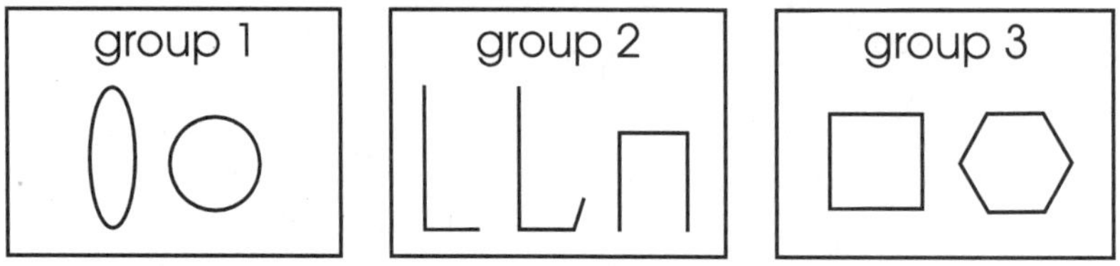

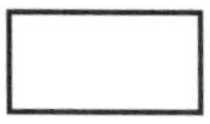

group 1 group 2 group 3

In which group does ▭ belong?

a group 1   **b** group 2   **c** group 3   **d** none of these choices

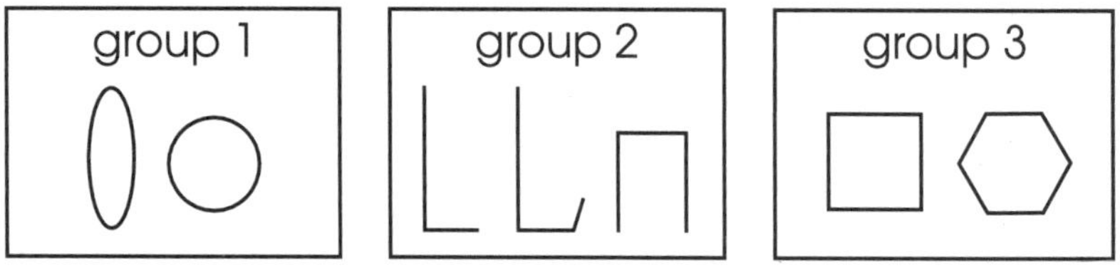

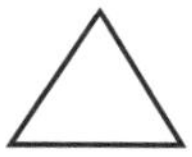

group 1 group 2 group 3

In which group does △ belong?

a group 1   **b** group 2   **c** group 3   **d** none of these choices

<table>
<tr><td>group 1

44, 55, 77</td><td>group 2

8, 6, 12</td><td>group 3

5, 10, 15</td></tr>
</table>

In which group does the number 33 belong?

ⓐ group 1   **ⓑ** group 2   **ⓒ** group 3   **ⓓ** none of these choices

<table>
<tr><td>group 1

10, 30, 50</td><td>group 2

61, 91, 121</td><td>group 3

11, 22, 33</td></tr>
</table>

In which group does the number 31 belong?

ⓐ group 1   **ⓑ** group 2   **ⓒ** group 3   **ⓓ** none of these choices

<table>
<tr><td>group 1

25, 50, 75</td><td>group 2

9, 18, 27</td><td>group 3

12, 24, 36</td></tr>
</table>

In which group does the number 100 belong?

ⓐ group 1   **ⓑ** group 2   **ⓒ** group 3   **ⓓ** none of these choices

If each bird lays three eggs, how many eggs will two birds lay?

   (a) 2   **(b)** 4   **(c)** 6   **(d)** 8

EXTEND THE THINKING: Write a number sentence that shows how you solved the problem.

If each bird lays three eggs, how many eggs will five birds lay?

   (a) 20   **(b)** 15   **(c)** 10   **(d)** 45

EXTEND THE THINKING: Write a number sentence that shows how you solved the problem.

If each bird lays three eggs, how many eggs will twelve birds lay?

   (a) 36   **(b)** 30   **(c)** 23   **(d)** 45

EXTEND THE THINKING: Write a number sentence that shows how you solved the problem.

If Sue has three balloons in each hand,
how many balloons is she holding?

(a) 3 (b) 6 (c) 5 (d) 30

If Sue has seven balloons in each hand,
how many balloons is she holding?

(a) 7 (b) 16 (c) 15 (d) 14

If Sue has eleven balloons in each hand,
how many balloons is she holding?

(a) 15 (b) 26 (c) 22 (d) 14

Section Answers
Patterns, Functions, and Algebra

Correct answers are shaded.

	page 7	page 8	page 9	page 10	page 11
○	**a** b c d	**a** b c d	a **b** c d	a **b** c d	a b c **d**
△	**a** b c d	a **b** c d	**a** b c d	a b c **d**	a **b** c d
▢	a **b** c d	**a** b c d	a **b** c d	**a** b c d	a b **c** d

	page 12	page 13	page 14	page 15	page 16
○	a b **c** d	a **b** c d	**a** b c d	a **b** c d	a b c **d**
△	a **b** c d	a b **c** d	a **b** c d	a **b** c d	**a** b c d
▢	**a** b c d	a **b** c d	**a** b c d	a **b** c d	**a** b c d

	page 17	page 18	page 19	page 20	page 21
○	**a** b c d	**a** b c d	**a** b c d	a b **c** d	a **b** c d
△	a **b** c d	a b **c** d	a **b** c d	a **b** c d	a b c **d**
▢	**a** b c d	a b **c** d	**a** b c d	**a** b c d	a b **c** d

Data Analysis and Probability

The *Level D* Data Analysis and Probability standards require students to

- collect, compare, contrast, and analyze data (information)

- identify the important and unimportant information in a problem

- make assumptions and inferences based on information

- recognize and apply the likelihood of outcomes based on number, size, and application (the manner in which the elements are arranged or chosen)

- understand and apply the idea of probability

Daily Sports Statistics

Have students bring in a statistics page of the newspaper sports section (e.g., basketball stats). Tape the pages to a board or wall, and discuss changes that occur in the statistics. Encourage students to analyze the data and make predictions of the probability of various scenarios such as the following:

- improving a point average by a given amount
- changing an average (e.g., increasing a batting average, lowering a handicap)
- winning future games/tournaments

Weekly Probability

Incorporate a weekly probability activity across the curriculum, such as the number of absences for the week. Discuss the probability of the number decreasing the following week. Discuss factors such as weather, holidays, or illness that might influence the results.

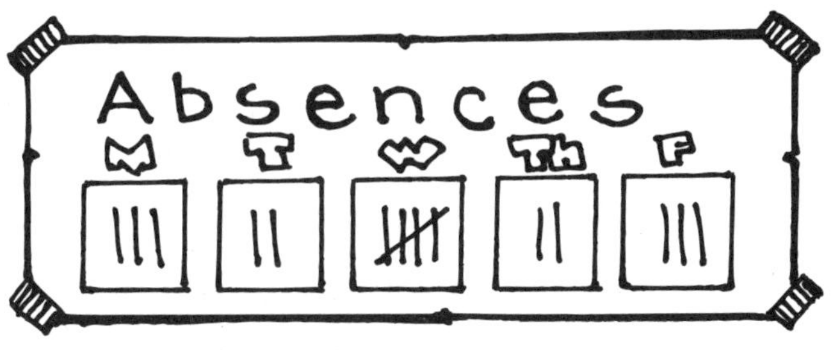

TEST-TAKING TIPS
FOR STUDENTS

✔ Use common sense. Disregard the obviously incorrect choices; then consider the remaining answers to find the "best" choice.

✔ Don't rush—carefully consider the choices that are very similar.

TEACHING TIP
FOR THIS SECTION

Tell students that they can sometimes more easily solve a probability problem if they determine the variable that influences the outcome. For example, have students examine the spinner in the ● problem on page 26. Explain that because the area for the number 5 is significantly greater than the area for the other two numbers, the arrow is more likely to land on the 5 (*d*).

→ Answers are on page 40.

Concepts: Data Analysis and Probability

Math Concept	Problem Set														
	page 25	page 26	page 27	page 28	page 29	page 30	page 31	page 32	page 33	page 34	page 35	page 36	page 37	page 38	page 39
Probability	X	X	X	X											
Data Analysis					X	X	X	X	X	X	X	X	X	X	X
Money											X				X
Pictographs								X							
Circle Graphs		X	X											X	
Tables	X				X	X	X			X	X				X
Multiplication							X	X	X						X
Addition/Subtraction					X	X	X	X	X		X	X		X	X
Bar Graphs									X			X	X		

Coins in a Bag

Pennies	Nickels	Dimes	Quarters
1	3	2	4

You choose one of these coins from a bag without looking. Which coin are you most likely to choose?

(a) quarter   (b) nickel   (c) dime   (d) penny

EXTEND THE THINKING: Which coin are you least likely to choose?

a

Coins in a Bag

Pennies	Nickels	Dimes	Quarters
4	12	13	4

You choose one of these coins from a bag without looking. Which coin are you most likely to choose?

(a) quarter   (b) nickel   (c) dime   (d) penny

EXTEND THE THINKING: Which coins are you least likely to choose?

c

Coins in a Bag

Pennies	Nickels	Dimes	Quarters
14	23	22	15

You choose one of these coins from a bag without looking. Which coin are you most likely to choose?

(a) quarter   (b) nickel   (c) dime   (d) penny

EXTEND THE THINKING: Which coin are you least likely to choose?

b

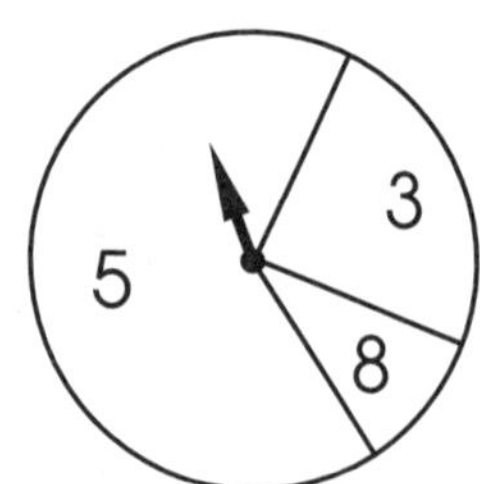

If you spin, on which number are you most likely to land?

(a) 3   (b) 8   (c) 7   (d) 5

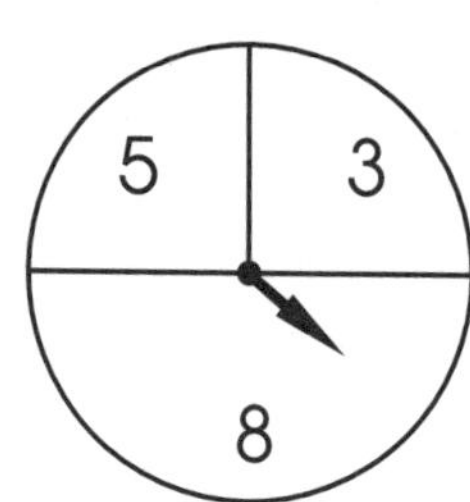

If you spin, on which number are you most likely to land?

(a) 3   (b) 8   (c) 7   (d) 5

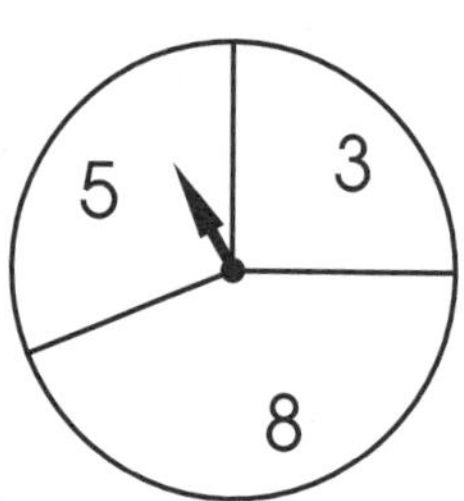

If you spin, on which number are you most likely to land?

(a) 3   (b) 8   (c) 7   (d) 5

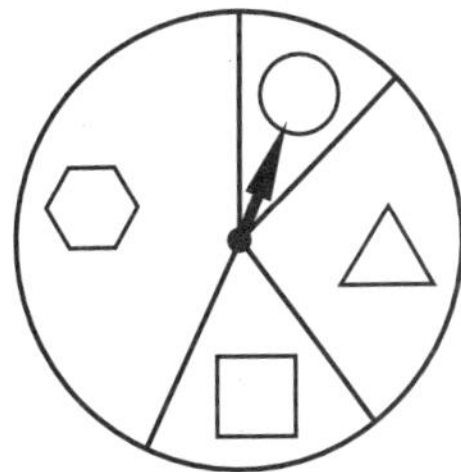

You are playing a board game with this spinner. If you spin, on which shape are you most likely to land?

ⓐ hexagon   **ⓑ** square   **ⓒ** triangle   **ⓓ** circle

EXTEND THE THINKING: On which shape are you least likely to land?

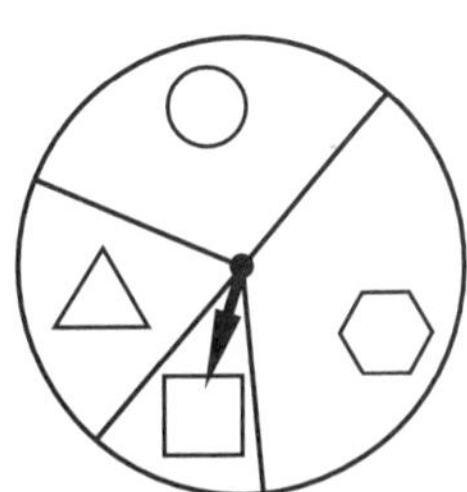

You are playing a board game with this spinner. If you spin, on which shape are you most likely to land?

ⓐ hexagon   **ⓑ** square   **ⓒ** triangle   **ⓓ** circle

EXTEND THE THINKING: On which shape are you least likely to land?

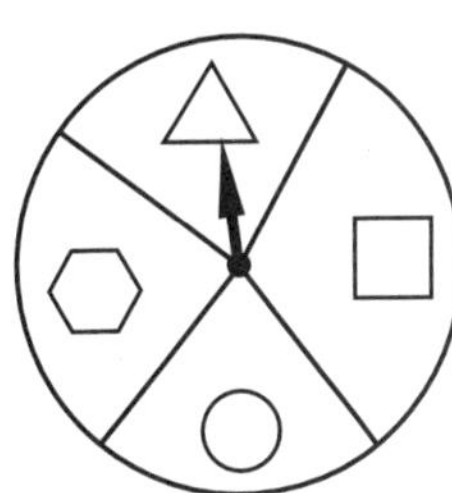

You are playing a board game with this spinner. If you spin, on which shape are you most likely to land?

ⓐ hexagon   **ⓑ** square   **ⓒ** triangle   **ⓓ** circle

EXTEND THE THINKING: Explain why you made that choice.

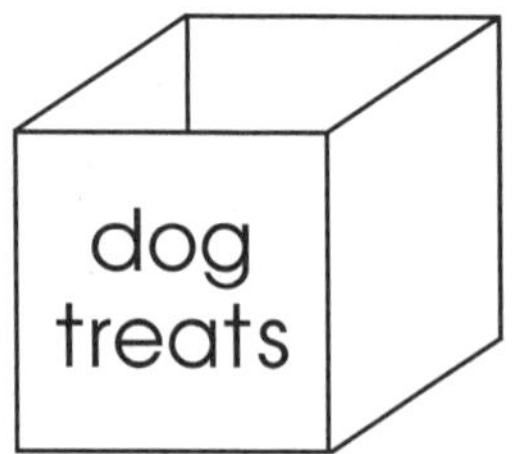

You want to give your dog one dog treat. The box has 15 green treats, 12 yellow treats, and 18 brown treats. Which color treat are you most likely to choose?

ⓐ orange   **ⓑ** green   **ⓒ** yellow   **ⓓ** brown

EXTEND THE THINKING: Which color treat are you least likely to choose?

You want to give your dog one dog treat. The box has 36 green treats, 42 orange treats, and 39 brown treats. Which color treat are you most likely to choose?

ⓐ orange   **ⓑ** green   **ⓒ** red   **ⓓ** brown

EXTEND THE THINKING: Which color treat are you least likely to choose?

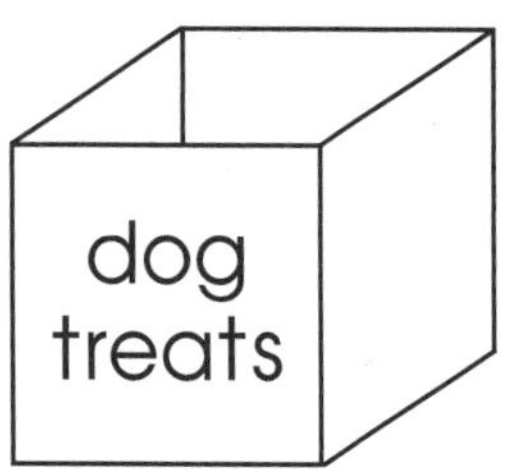

You want to give your dog one dog treat. The box has 45 green treats, 46 yellow treats, and 48 brown treats. Which color treat are you most likely to choose?

ⓐ orange   **ⓑ** green   **ⓒ** yellow   **ⓓ** brown

EXTEND THE THINKING: Which color treat are you least likely to choose?

Rabbit Weight

Week 1	8 ounces
Week 2	12 ounces
Week 3	18 ounces
Week 4	22 ounces

How much weight did the rabbit gain between weeks 1 and 2?

(a) 2 pounds   **(b)** 4 ounces   **(c)** 4 pounds   **(d)** 10 ounces

EXTEND THE THINKING: Write a number sentence that shows how you solved the problem.

Rabbit Weight

Week 1	8 ounces
Week 2	12 ounces
Week 3	18 ounces
Week 4	22 ounces

How much weight did the rabbit gain between weeks 1 and 3?

(a) 2 pounds   **(b)** 4 ounces   **(c)** 4 pounds   **(d)** 10 ounces

EXTEND THE THINKING: Write a number sentence that shows how you solved the problem.

Rabbit Weight

Week 1	8 ounces
Week 2	12 ounces
Week 3	18 ounces
Week 4	22 ounces

Between which two weeks did the rabbit gain the most weight?

(a) week 1 and week 2   **(b)** week 2 and week 3   **(c)** week 3 and week 4   **(d)** week 4 and week 5

EXTEND THE THINKING: Explain how you solved the problem.

Books Read

First Grade	Second Grade	Third Grade
559	528	598

The library is having a reading contest. Which grade has read the greatest number of books so far?

ⓐ kindergarten   **ⓑ** first grade   **ⓒ** second grade   **ⓓ** third grade

EXTEND THE THINKING: Write a number sentence that shows how you solved the problem.

Books Read

First Grade	Second Grade	Third Grade
559	528	598

The library is having a reading contest. How many more books have the third graders read than the second graders?

ⓐ 40   **ⓑ** 75   **ⓒ** 45   **ⓓ** 70

EXTEND THE THINKING: Write a number sentence that shows how you solved the problem.

Books Read

First Grade	Second Grade	Third Grade
559	528	598

The library is having a reading contest. If the first graders read 40 more books, who will win the contest?

ⓐ kindergarten   **ⓑ** first grade   **ⓒ** second grade   **ⓓ** third grade

EXTEND THE THINKING: Write a number sentence that shows how you solved the problem.

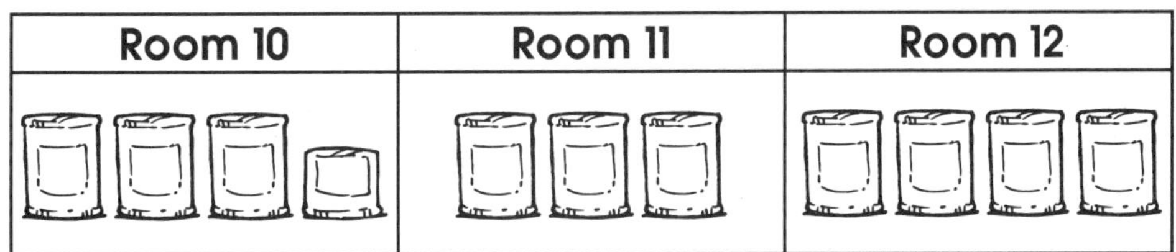

**Each can represents ten cans for a food drive.
Which class donated the greatest number of cans?**

ⓐ Room 15   **ⓑ** Room 11   **ⓒ** Room 12   **ⓓ** Room 10

EXTEND THE THINKING: Explain how you solved the problem.

**Each can represents ten cans for a food drive.
How many cans did Room 10 donate?**

ⓐ 40   **ⓑ** 45   **ⓒ** 30   **ⓓ** 35

EXTEND THE THINKING: Explain how you solved the problem.

**Each can represents 20 cans for a food drive.
How many cans did Room 10 donate?**

ⓐ 35   **ⓑ** 80   **ⓒ** 65   **ⓓ** 70

EXTEND THE THINKING: Explain how you solved the problem.

You want to make a pictograph that shows how many cookies you eat in one week. Which answer best explains what a cookie picture would represent on your pictograph?

ⓐ each cookie you eat

ⓑ each cookie in your cookie jar

ⓒ each cookie you don't eat

ⓓ each gumdrop you eat instead

EXTEND THE THINKING: Explain why you made that choice.

You want to make a pictograph that shows how many cookies you eat in one week. Which answer best explains what half of a cookie picture would represent on your pictograph?

ⓐ each cookie you eat

ⓑ each half of a cookie in your cookie jar

ⓒ each cookie you don't eat

ⓓ each half of a cookie you eat

EXTEND THE THINKING: Explain why you made that choice.

You want to track how many cookies you eat in one week. If one cookie represents every five cookies eaten, how many did you eat if you draw five cookies?

ⓐ 5　　　ⓑ 10　　　ⓒ 25　　　ⓓ 50

EXTEND THE THINKING: Write a number sentence that shows how you solved the problem.

Candy Bars Sold

Each shaded box represents one candy bar you have sold. If you want to sell ten candy bars, how many more do you need to sell?

10
9
8
7
6
5
4
3
2
1

(a) 2   **(b)** 10   **(c)** 7   **(d)** 1

Candy Bars Sold

Each shaded box represents five candy bars you have sold. If you want to sell 50 candy bars, how many more do you need to sell?

(a) 50   **(b)** 10   **(c)** 8   **(d)** 40

Candy Bars Sold

Each shaded box represents ten candy bars you have sold. If you want to sell 100 candy bars, how many more do you need to sell?

(a) 50   **(b)** 5   **(c)** 100   **(d)** 70

TV Schedule

channel	8:30	9:00	9:30
22	Look	Wild Animals	Catch
26	Captured	Web Wizards	Soccer
27	Shipwrecks	Blast Off	Brainiacs

Which show can you watch at 9:30?

ⓐ Look   **ⓑ** Catch   **ⓒ** Web Wizards   **ⓓ** Dynamite Doggies

TV Schedule

channel	8:30	9:00	9:30
22	Look	Wild Animals	Catch
26	Captured	Web Wizards	Soccer
27	Shipwrecks	Blast Off	Brainiacs

At what time can you watch Shipwrecks?

ⓐ 8:00   **ⓑ** 9:00   **ⓒ** 9:30   **ⓓ** 8:30

TV Schedule

channel	8:30	9:00	9:30
22	Look	Wild Animals	Catch
26	Captured	Web Wizards	Soccer
27	Shipwrecks	Blast Off	Brainiacs

When Web Wizards ends, which show begins on the same channel?

ⓐ Soccer   **ⓑ** Catch   **ⓒ** Captured   **ⓓ** Brainiacs

Mathematical Thinking: Level D © 2001 Creative Teaching Press

Which two items can you buy for exactly $2.00?

(a) bacon and fruit

(b) fruit and pancakes

(c) pancakes and waffles

(d) bacon and pancakes

Which two items can you buy for exactly $2.25?

(a) bacon and fruit

(b) fruit and pancakes

(c) pancakes and waffles

(d) bacon and pancakes

How much does it cost to eat pancakes, fruit, and bacon?

(a) $1.75

(b) $3.75

(c) $3.25

(d) $2.75

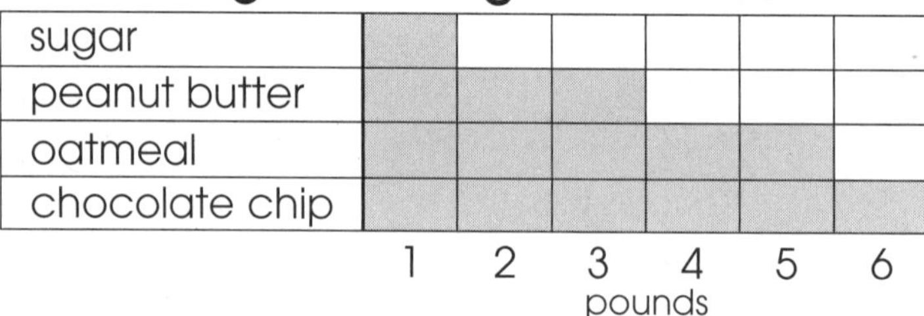

Weight of a Bag of Cookies

	sugar					
sugar	░					
peanut butter	░	░	░			
oatmeal	░	░	░	░	░	
chocolate chip	░	░	░	░	░	░

1 2 3 4 5 6
pounds

Which bag of cookies is the heaviest?

ⓐ sugar   **ⓑ** oatmeal   **ⓒ** chocolate chip   **ⓓ** peanut butter

EXTEND THE THINKING: Which bag is the lightest?

Weight of a Bag of Cookies

sugar	░					
peanut butter	░	░				
oatmeal	░	░	░	░	░	
chocolate chip	░	░	░	░	░	░

1 2 3 4 5 6
pounds

How much heavier is a bag of oatmeal cookies than a bag of sugar cookies?

ⓐ 4 pounds   **ⓑ** 4 ounces   **ⓒ** 5 pounds   **ⓓ** 5 ounces

EXTEND THE THINKING: Write a number sentence that shows how you solved the problem. 

Weight of a Bag of Cookies

sugar	░					
peanut butter	░	░	░			
oatmeal	░	░	░			
chocolate chip	░	░	░	░	░	░

1 2 3 4 5 6
pounds

A bag of gingersnaps weighs twice as much as a bag of peanut butter cookies. The weight of the bag of gingersnaps equals the weight of which other bag of cookies?

ⓐ sugar   **ⓑ** oatmeal   **ⓒ** chocolate chip   **ⓓ** peanut butter

EXTEND THE THINKING: Write a number sentence that shows how you solved the problem. 

Six people were asked what their favorite number is between 1–20. If your favorite number is 16, in which column would it go?

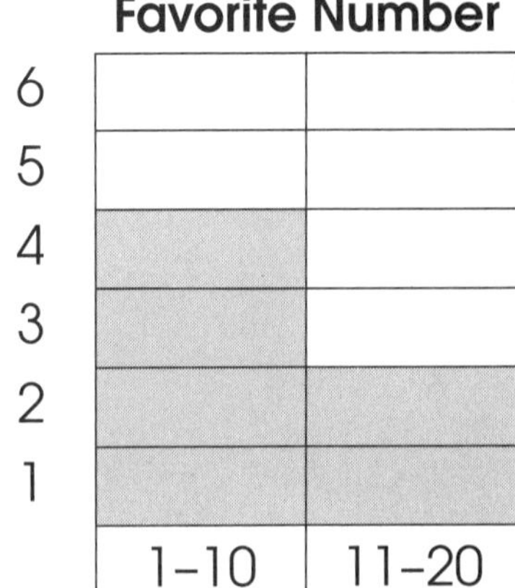

(a) 1–10   **(b)** 11–20   **(c)** 1–20   **(d)** 1–15

EXTEND THE THINKING: Explain how you solved the problem.

Six people were asked what their favorite number is between 1–20. If your favorite number is 8, in which column would it go?

(a) 1–10   **(b)** 11–20   **(c)** 1–20   **(d)** 1–15

EXTEND THE THINKING: Explain how you solved the problem.

Six people were asked what their favorite number is between 1–20. What is the range of numbers?

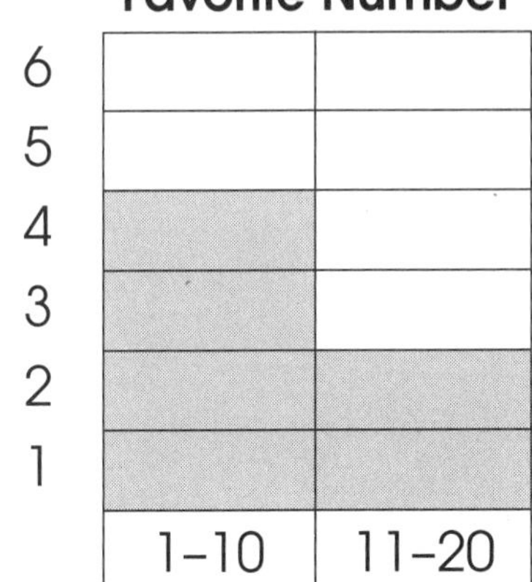

(a) 1–30   **(b)** 11–20   **(c)** 1–20   **(d)** 1–50

EXTEND THE THINKING: Explain how you solved the problem.

Favorite Color

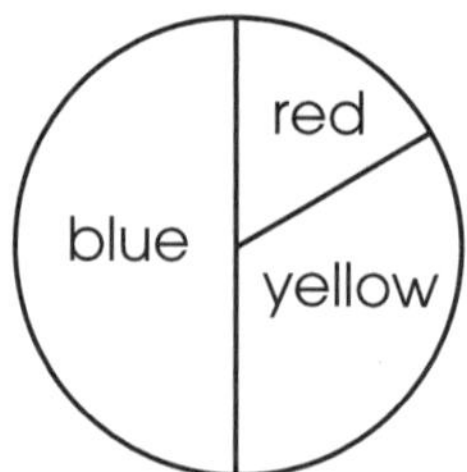

Which color is the most popular?

ⓐ red   **ⓑ** yellow   **ⓒ** green   **ⓓ** blue

EXTEND THE THINKING: Which color is the least popular?

Favorite Color

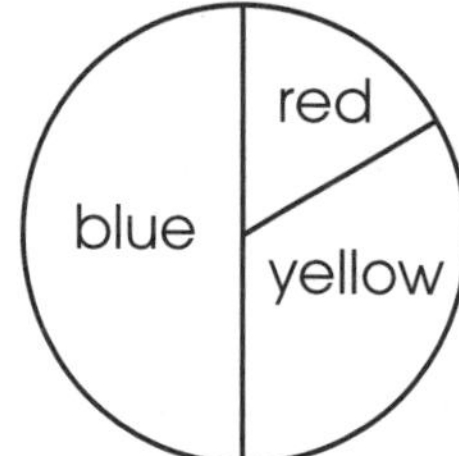

If two people chose red, how many people do you think chose blue?

ⓐ 3   **ⓑ** 4   **ⓒ** 6   **ⓓ** 2

EXTEND THE THINKING: How many people do you think chose yellow?

Favorite Color

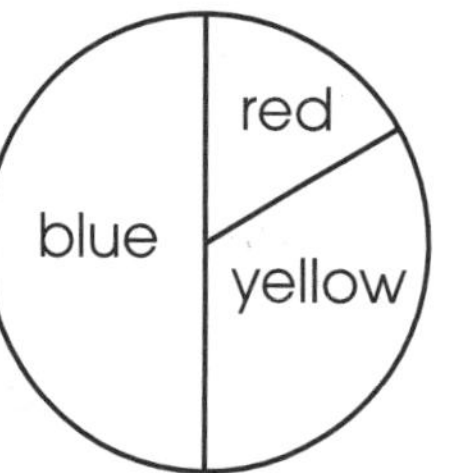

If ten people chose yellow, how many people do you think chose blue?

ⓐ 15   **ⓑ** 10   **ⓒ** 20   **ⓓ** 25

EXTEND THE THINKING: How many people do you think chose red?

Apple Sale

Number	Cost
2	$1.00
5	$2.00
10	$3.00
25	$5.00

How many apples can you buy with $3.00?

(a) 1   (b) 5   (c) 10   (d) 25

Apple Sale

Number	Cost
2	$1.00
5	$2.00
10	$3.00
25	$5.00

How many apples can you buy with $10.00?

(a) 10   (b) 50   (c) 35   (d) 75

Apple Sale

Number	Cost
2	$1.00
5	$2.00
10	$3.00
25	$5.00

You want to buy exactly 20 apples.
What is the least expensive way to buy them?

(a) 4 bags of 5   (b) 1 bag of 25   (c) 2 bags of 10   (d) 10 bags of 2

Section Answers
Data Analysis and Probability

Correct answers are shaded.

	page 25	page 26	page 27	page 28	page 29
○	**a** b c d	a b c **d**	**a** b c d	a b c **d**	a **b** c d
△	a b **c** d	a **b** c d	**a** b c d	**a** b c d	a b c **d**
□	a **b** c d	a **b** c d	a **b** c d	a b c **d**	a **b** c d

	page 30	page 31	page 32	page 33	page 34
○	a b c **d**	a b **c** d	**a** b c d	**a** b c d	a **b** c d
△	a b c **d**	a b c **d**	a b c **d**	a **b** c d	a b c **d**
□	a **b** c d	a b c **d**	a b **c** d	**a** b c d	**a** b c d

	page 35	page 36	page 37	page 38	page 39
○	a **b** c d	a b **c** d	a **b** c d	a b c **d**	a b **c** d
△	a b c **d**	**a** b c d	**a** b c d	a b **c** d	a **b** c d
□	a b c **d**	a b **c** d	a b **c** d	**a** b c d	a b **c** d

Geometry and Spatial Relationships

The *Level D* Geometry and Spatial Relationships standards require students to

- identify, compare, and contrast shapes and solids

- compare attributes of a shape such as the number of sides, angles, or corners

- identify real-life objects that share the same attributes as a given geometric shape

- identify a line of symmetry

- make a design symmetrical by creating a mirrored image

- complete spatial design tasks

Geometric Art

Cut out for each student several different-colored construction paper shapes in a variety of sizes. For example, give each student four circles, four squares, four triangles, and four rectangles all in different colors and sizes. Give each student a piece of white construction paper, and ask students to glue their shapes onto their paper to create a picture. Have students label each shape in their picture, and then invite them to share their "shape picture" with the class.

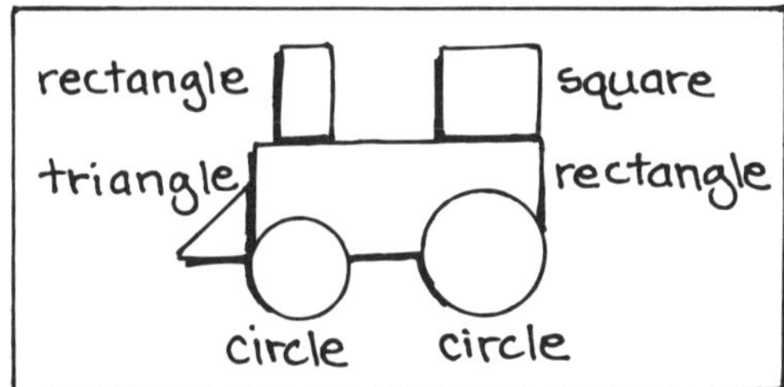

Symmetry Drawings

Have students cut out symmetrical pictures from catalogs or magazines (e.g., items of clothing, pieces of sports equipment). Collect the pictures, cut them in half, glue them onto separate pieces of paper, and laminate them. Give half of a picture and wipe-off crayons to each student, and encourage students to complete the picture by drawing the mirrored image.

TEST-TAKING TIPS FOR STUDENTS

✔ Avoid selecting answers that are unfamiliar or that you do not understand.

✔ Answer those questions you know first; leave challenging ones for later.

✔ Don't change your answers without good reason.

TEACHING TIP FOR THIS SECTION

Tell students that they can sometimes more easily solve a geometry problem if they draw an illustration of a described shape. For example, have students draw an illustration that matches the description in the ● problem on page 45. Explain that a rectangle best matches the description of the shape (c).

→ Answers are on page 58.

Concepts: Geometry and Spatial Relationships

Math Concept	Problem Set	page 43	page 44	page 45	page 46	page 47	page 48	page 49	page 50	page 51	page 52	page 53	page 54	page 55	page 56	page 57
Symmetry							X		X	X						
Shapes		X	X	X							X	X	X	X		X
Solids					X	X									X	
Spatial Relationships			X					X	X	X						
Properties of Shapes/Solids				X	X							X	X			
Addition/Subtraction		X				X					X	X	X	X	X	
Transformations								X								
Measurement													X	X	X	
Multiplication											X	X				
Congruency									X	X						X

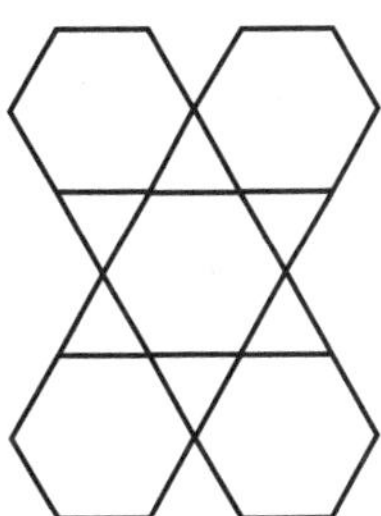

Which shape appears more frequently in the picture?

(a) rectangle   **(b)** hexagon   **(c)** triangle   **(d)** square

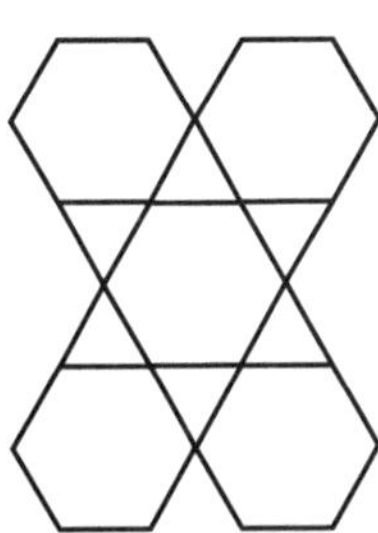

How many more small triangles are there than hexagons?

(a) 8   **(b)** 2   **(c)** 1   **(d)** 5

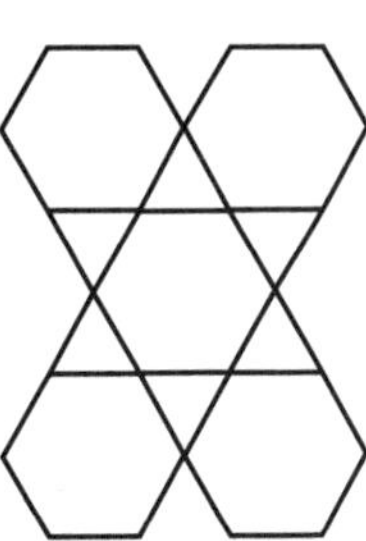

You want to add to the picture twice as many rectangles as hexagons. How many rectangles will you add?

(a) 3   **(b)** 6   **(c)** 10   **(d)** 8

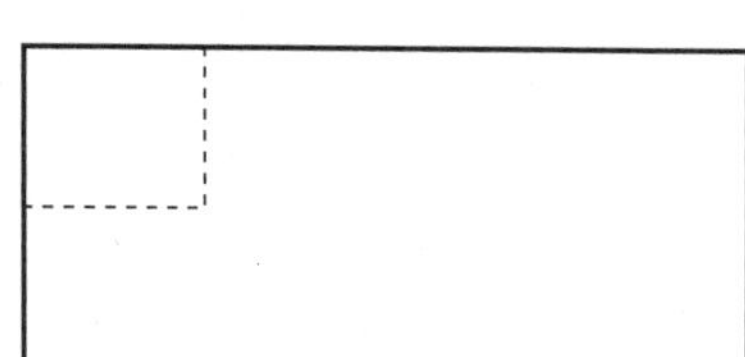

How many small rectangles can fit into the large rectangle?

(a) 2   (b) 6   (c) 4   (d) 7

EXTEND THE THINKING: How many angles will there be when the small rectangles are in the large rectangle?

How many squares can fit into the rectangle?

(a) 8   (b) 6   (c) 5   (d) 7

EXTEND THE THINKING: How many straight sides will there be when the squares are in the rectangle?

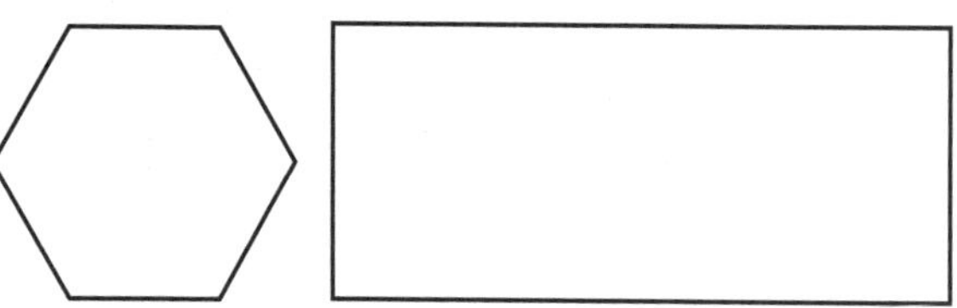

How many hexagons can fit into the rectangle?

(a) 2   (b) 3   (c) 4   (d) 5

EXTEND THE THINKING: How many triangles will there be when the hexagons are in the rectangle?

Mathematical Thinking: Level D © 2001 Creative Teaching Press

What is the name of the shape?

*I have four sides.
Two of my sides can be longer
than the other sides.
I have four right angles.*

ⓐ circle   **ⓑ** square   **ⓒ** rectangle   **ⓓ** triangle

EXTEND THE THINKING: What do you have in your room that is the same shape?

What is the name of the shape?

*I am a closed figure.
I have no straight sides.
Every part of me is the same
distance from the center.*

ⓐ circle   **ⓑ** square   **ⓒ** rectangle   **ⓓ** triangle

EXTEND THE THINKING: What do you have in your room that is the same shape?

What is the name of the shape?

*I am a quadrilateral.
I have only one pair of parallel sides.*

ⓐ hexagon   **ⓑ** triangle   **ⓒ** rectangle   **ⓓ** trapezoid

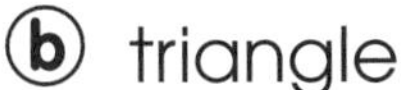**EXTEND THE THINKING:** What do you have in your room that is the same shape?

What is the name of the solid?

I have two faces that are circles.
I am the shape of a can.

ⓐ circle   **ⓑ** sphere   **ⓒ** cube   **ⓓ** cylinder

What is the name of the solid?

I am a pointed figure.
My base is round and flat.
I am the shape of a party hat.

ⓐ cylinder   **ⓑ** sphere   **ⓒ** cube   **ⓓ** cone

What is the name of the solid?

I have four triangular faces.
I have four points.

ⓐ cube   **ⓑ** triangular prism   **ⓒ** cone   **ⓓ** rectangular prism

How many cylinders do you see in the picture?

(a) 7   (b) 2   (c) 5   (d) 3

EXTEND THE THINKING: Write a number sentence that shows how many cones and cylinders there are.

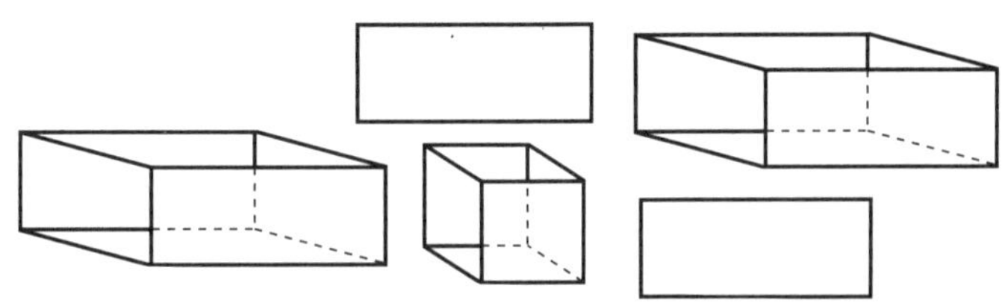

How many rectangular prisms do you see in the picture?

(a) 1   (b) 2   (c) 4   (d) 3

EXTEND THE THINKING: Write a number sentence that shows how many more rectangles than cubes there are.

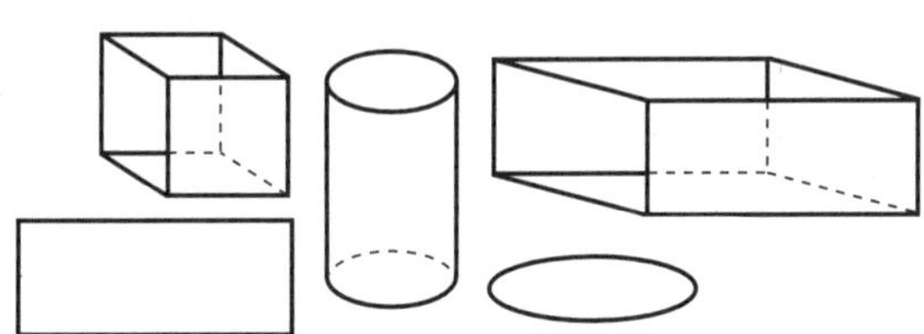

How many of the geometric figures are solids?

(a) 3   (b) 6   (c) 4   (d) 5

EXTEND THE THINKING: Write a number sentence that shows how many more solids than shapes there are.

Which picture shows a line of symmetry?

 a

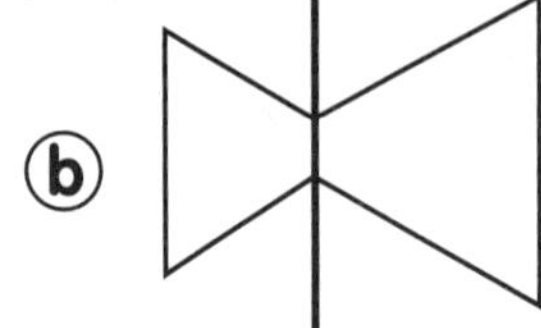 b

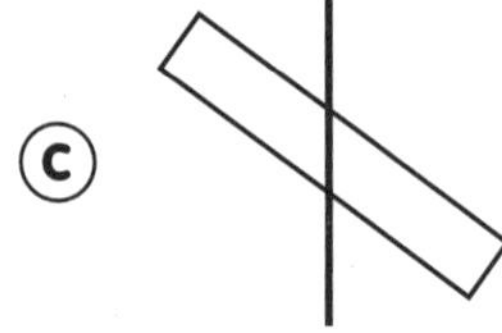 c

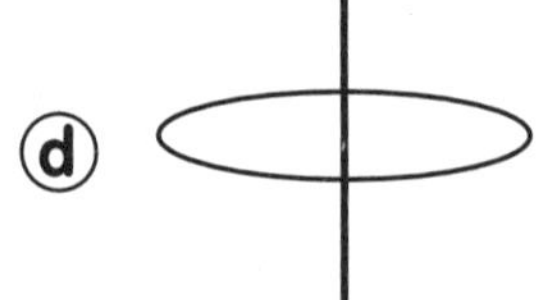 d

EXTEND THE THINKING: Explain why you made that choice.

Which picture shows a line of symmetry?

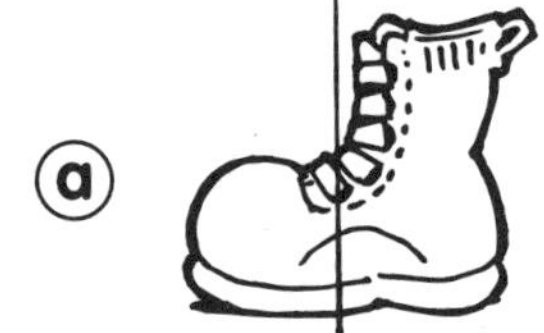 a

 b

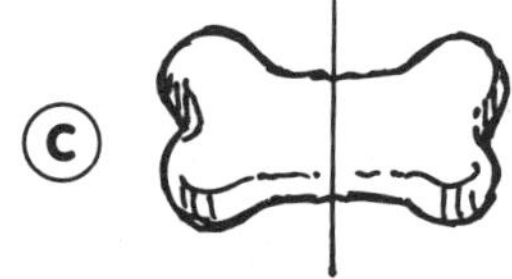 c

 d

EXTEND THE THINKING: Explain why you made that choice.

Which picture shows a line of symmetry?

 a

 b

 c

 d

EXTEND THE THINKING: Draw another line of symmetry on the answer.

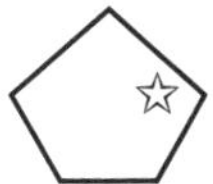

Which picture shows a slide to the right?

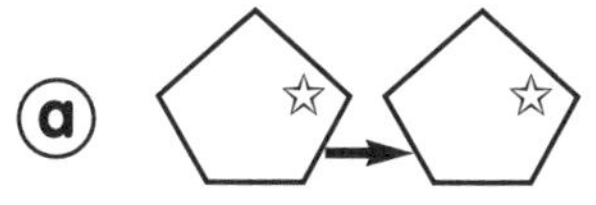
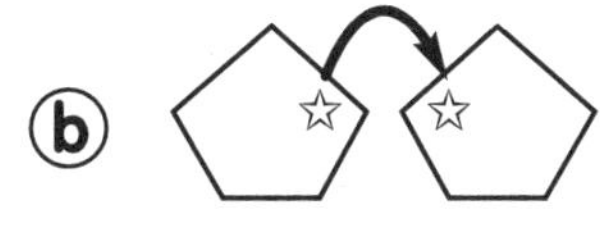

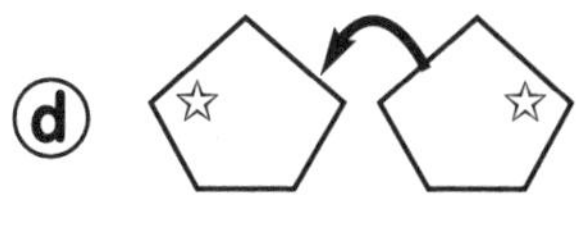

EXTEND THE THINKING: Explain why you made that choice.

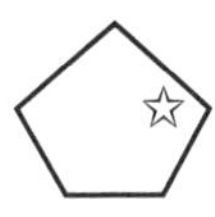

Which picture shows a rotation?

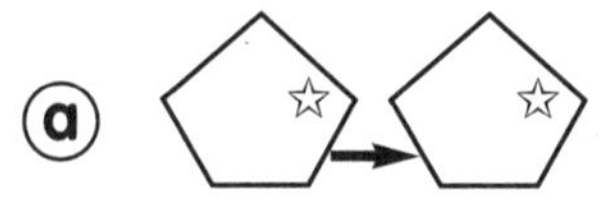
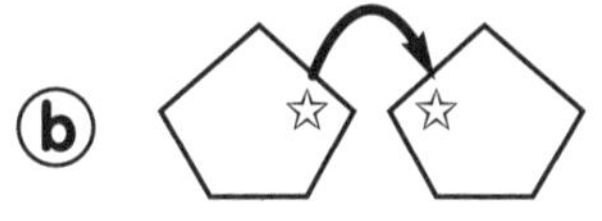
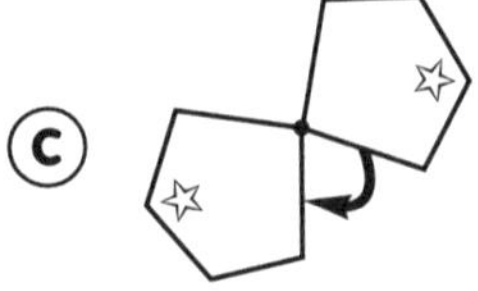
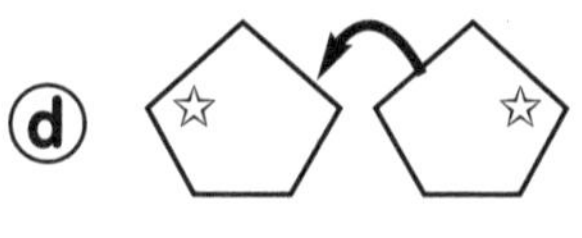

EXTEND THE THINKING: Explain why you made that choice.

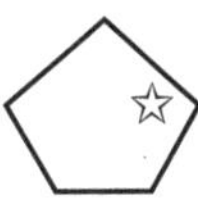

Which picture shows a reflection to the left?

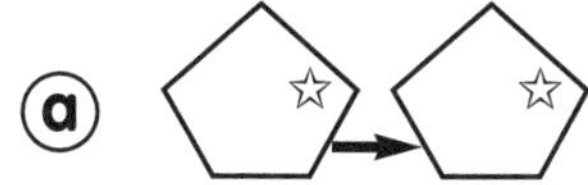
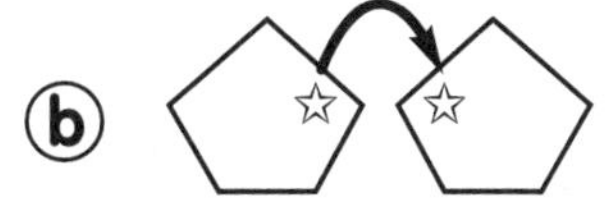
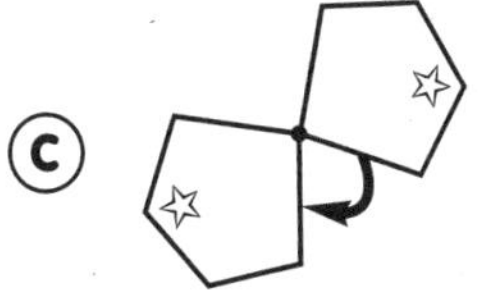
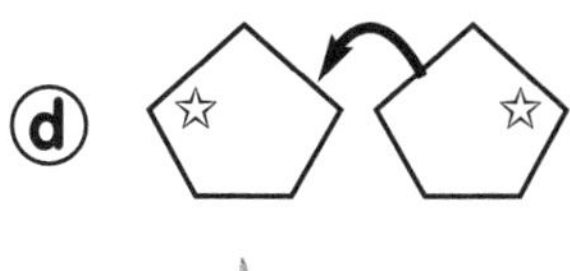

EXTEND THE THINKING: Explain why you made that choice.

Which piece is missing from the picture?

Which piece is missing from the picture?

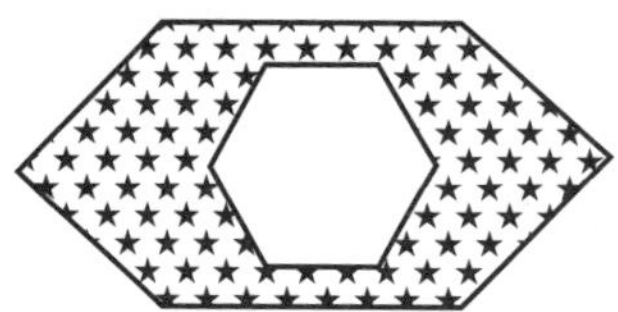

Which piece is missing from the picture?

  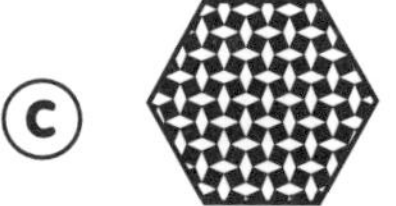 

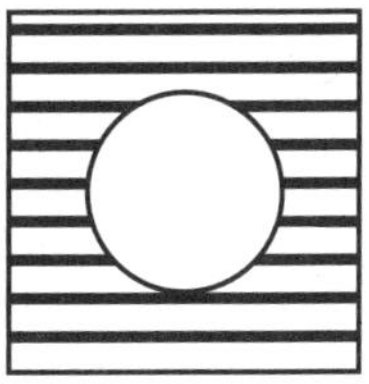

Which piece is missing from the picture?

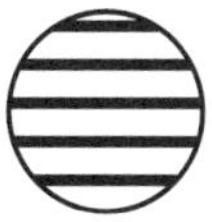

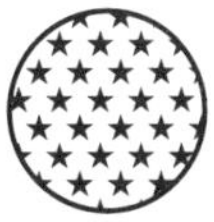

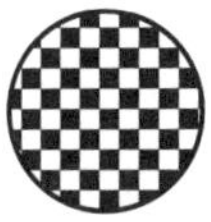

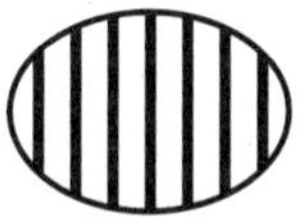

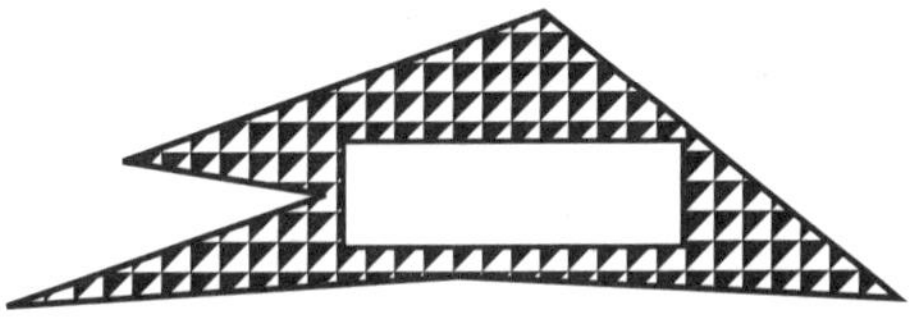

a   b   c   d

Which piece is missing from the picture?

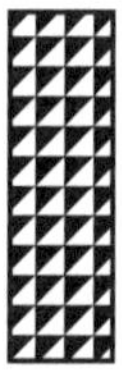

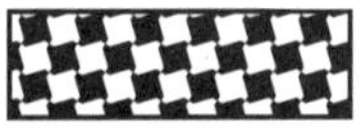

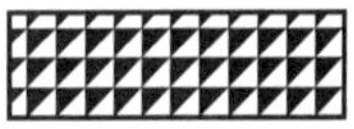

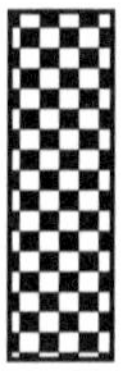

a   b   c   d

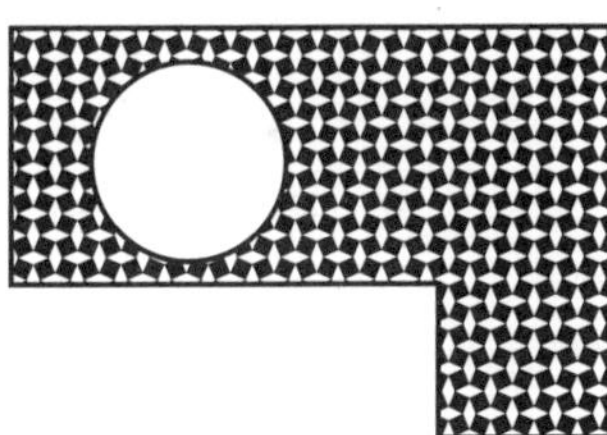

Which piece is missing from the picture?

 a   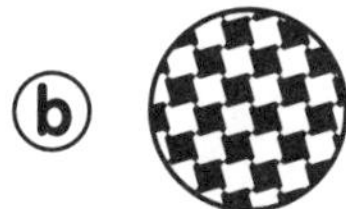 b   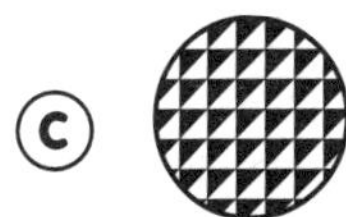 c   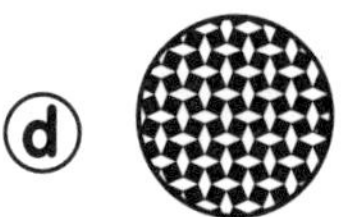 d

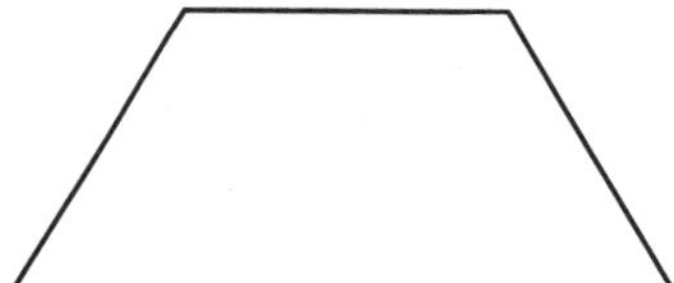

How many sides are on three separate rectangles?

(a) 4   **(b)** 8   **(c)** 16   **(d)** 12

How many sides are on five separate trapezoids?

(a) 20   **(b)** 25   **(c)** 12   **(d)** 30

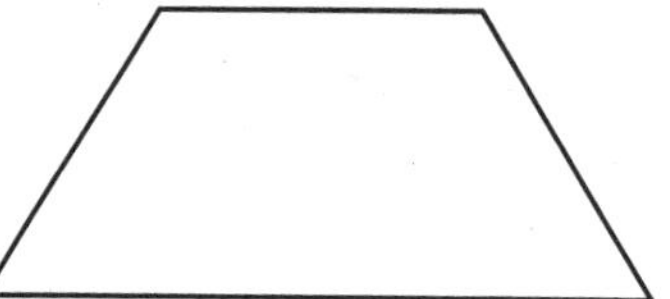

If there are 48 sides, how many trapezoids are there?

(a) 10   **(b)** 9   **(c)** 8   **(d)** 12

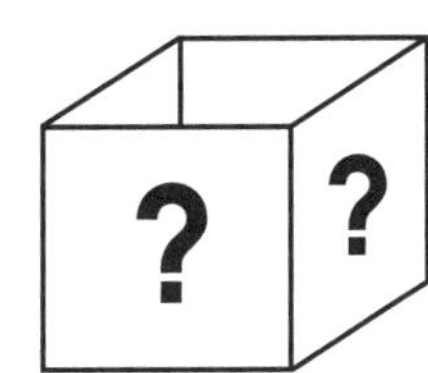

There are eight sides inside the Secret Shape Box. Which shapes could be inside?

(a) 2 triangles   (b) 2 circles   (c) 2 squares   (d) 2 cubes

EXTEND THE THINKING: Which other shapes could be inside?

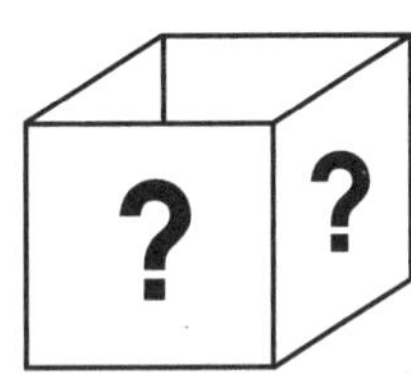

There are twelve sides inside the Secret Shape Box. Which shapes could be inside?

(a) 4 triangles   (b) 2 triangles   (c) 4 squares   (d) 2 rectangles

EXTEND THE THINKING: Which other shapes could be inside?

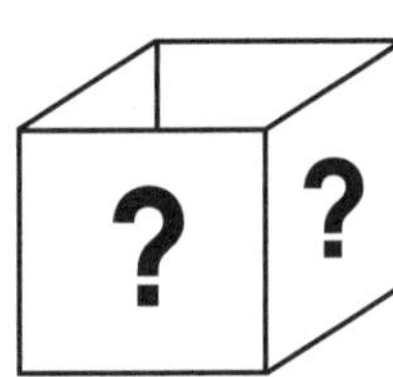

There are 24 sides inside the Secret Shape Box. Which shapes could be inside?

(a) 8 triangles   (b) 2 squares   (c) 8 squares   (d) 5 triangles

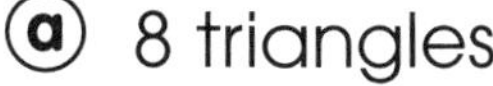

EXTEND THE THINKING: Which other shapes could be inside?

How many kilometers is it around two sides of the hexagon?

(a) 10 km **(b)** 50 km **(c)** 5 km **(d)** 20 km

EXTEND THE THINKING: How many kilometers is it around four sides?

How many kilometers is it around two sides of the hexagon?

(a) 10 km **(b)** 8 km **(c)** 80 km **(d)** 16 km

EXTEND THE THINKING: How many kilometers is it around four sides?

How many kilometers is it around half the distance of one side of the hexagon?

(a) 7 km **(b)** 3 km **(c)** $3\frac{1}{2}$ km **(d)** $5\frac{1}{2}$ km

EXTEND THE THINKING: How many kilometers is it all the way around the hexagon?

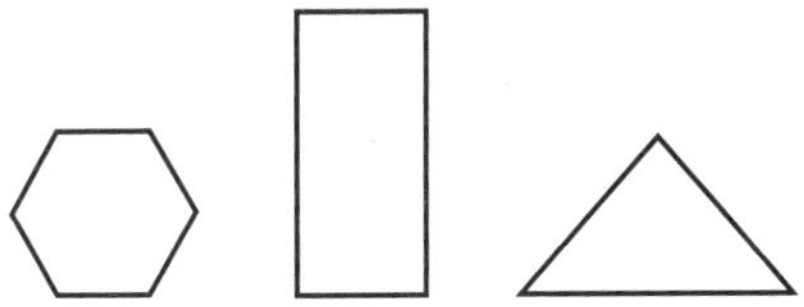

height: 35 in 57 in 23 in

Which shape is the shortest?

ⓐ hexagon ⓑ rectangle ⓒ triangle ⓓ square

EXTEND THE THINKING: Which shape is the tallest?

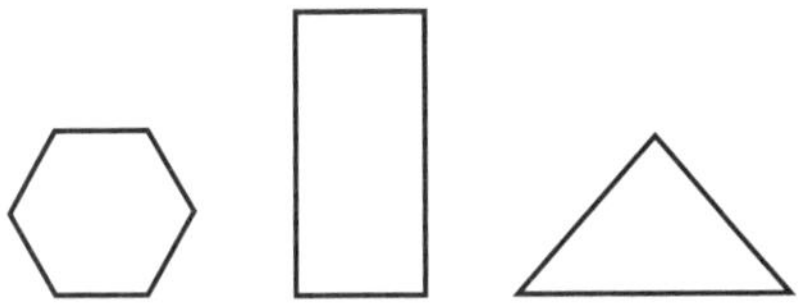

height: 35 in 57 in 23 in

If you stacked two hexagons, how tall would they be?

ⓐ 46 in ⓑ 35 in ⓒ 105 in ⓓ 70 in

EXTEND THE THINKING: Write a number sentence that shows how you solved the problem.

You stacked two shapes. They are 80 inches tall. Which shapes did you use?

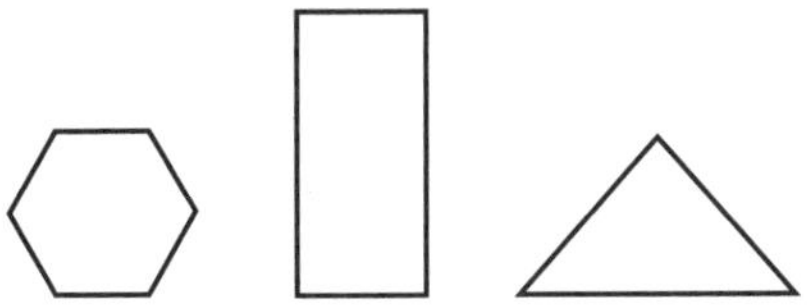

height: 35 in 57 in 23 in

ⓐ 1 hexagon and 1 triangle

ⓑ 2 triangles

ⓒ 1 rectangle and 1 triangle

ⓓ 2 hexagons

EXTEND THE THINKING: How tall would your stack be if you added one triangle?

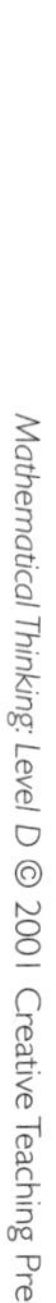

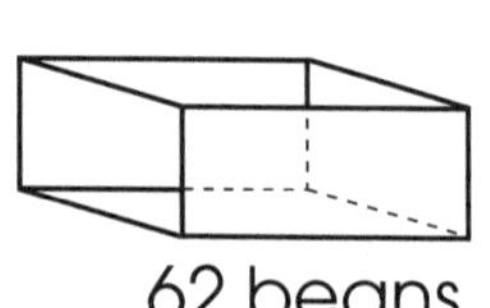  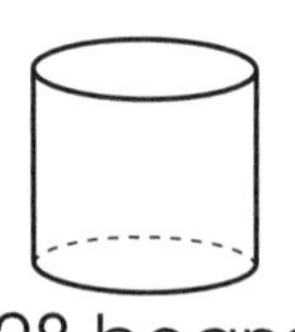

62 beans   24 beans   28 beans

Which container holds the fewest jelly beans?

ⓐ cylinder   **ⓑ** cone   **ⓒ** rectangular prism   **ⓓ** cube

62 beans   24 beans   28 beans

You want to store 58 jelly beans. Which container could you use?

ⓐ cylinder   **ⓑ** cone   **ⓒ** rectangular prism   **ⓓ** cube

If you want to store exactly 52 jelly beans, which containers could you use?

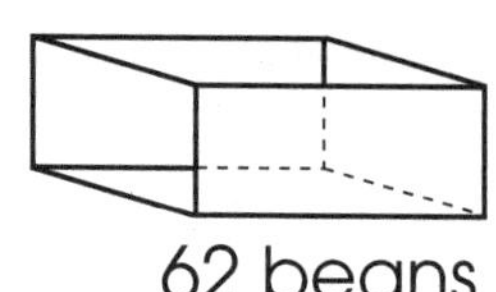 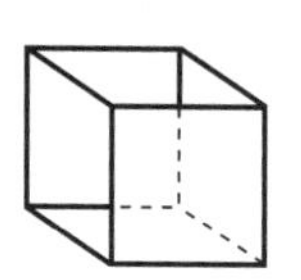 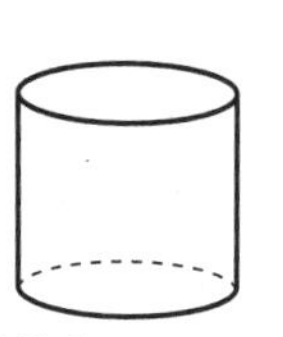

62 beans   24 beans   28 beans

ⓐ 1 cylinder and 1 cube

ⓑ 2 cubes

ⓒ 2 rectangular prisms

ⓓ 1 cube

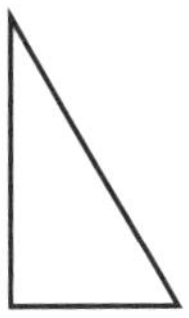

Which shape is not congruent to the picture?

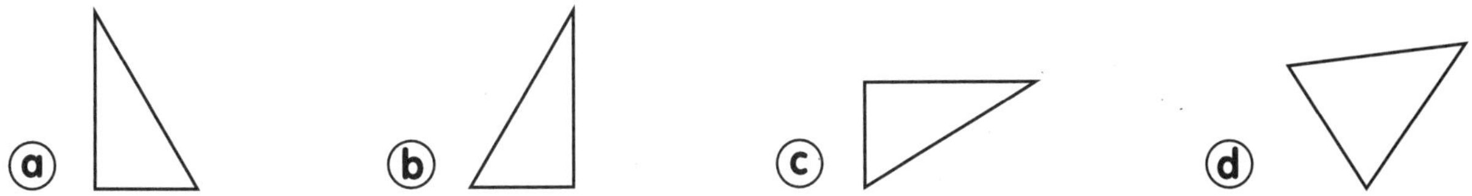

(a) (b) (c) (d)

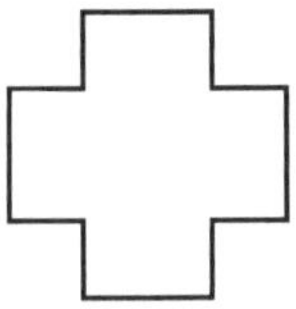

Which shape is not congruent to the picture?

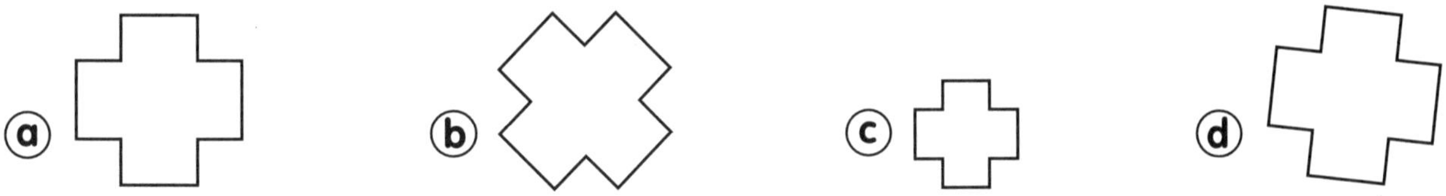

(a) (b) (c) (d)

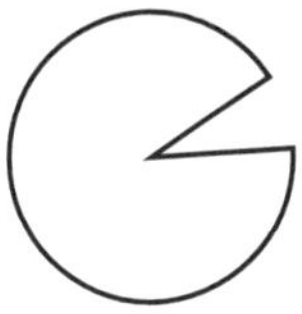

Which shape is not congruent to the picture?

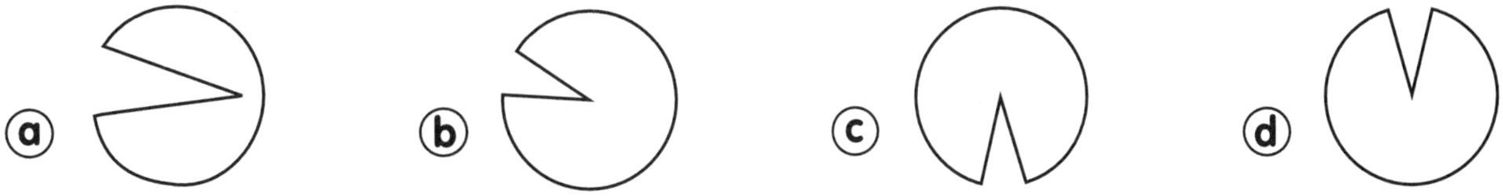

(a) (b) (c) (d)

Section Answers
Geometry and Spatial Relationships

Correct answers are shaded.

	page 43	page 44	page 45	page 46	page 47
○	a b **c** d	a b **c** d	a b **c** d	a b c **d**	a **b** c d
△	a b **c** d	**a** b c d	**a** b c d	a b c **d**	a **b** c d
□	a b **c** d	**a** b c d	a b c **d**	a **b** c d	**a** b c d

	page 48	page 49	page 50	page 51	page 52
○	a b c **d**	**a** b c d	a b **c** d	**a** b c d	a b c **d**
△	a b **c** d	a b **c** d	a **b** c d	a b **c** d	**a** b c d
□	a b c **d**	a b c **d**	a **b** c d	a b c **d**	a b c **d**

	page 53	page 54	page 55	page 56	page 57
○	a b **c** d	**a** b c d	a b **c** d	a **b** c d	a b c **d**
△	**a** b c d	a b c **d**	a b c **d**	a b **c** d	a b **c** d
□	**a** b c d	a b **c** d	a b **c** d	**a** b c d	**a** b c d

Logic and Critical Thinking

The *Level D* Logic and Critical Thinking standards require students to

- compare and contrast numbers

- identify odd/even and greater than/less than

- apply the concepts of place value

- apply a variety of strategies to solve problems and identify mystery numbers

- identify multiples and fractions of a number

Logic Riddles

In advance, show four students a set of red, blue, green, and yellow snap cubes, and have each student choose a favorite color from the set. Copy a class set of those four students' school photographs. Place each set of four photos in a bag with a set of the four different-colored snap cubes. Give each student in the class a bag, and write on the board or overhead projector clues about the four students and their favorite color. Challenge the class to correctly match each color to a photo. Discuss the solution as a class, and record students' reasoning on the board or overhead projector.

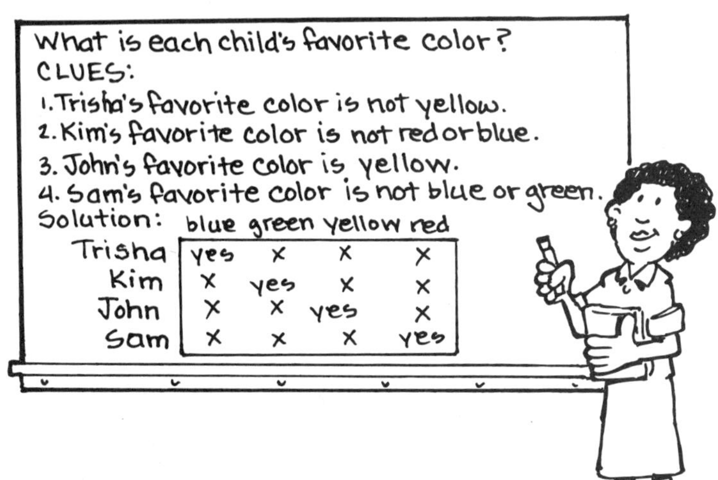

	blue	green	yellow	red
Trisha	yes	x	x	x
Kim	x	yes	x	x
John	x	x	yes	x
Sam	x	x	x	yes

→ Answers are on page 76.

Concepts: Logic and Critical Thinking

Math Concept	Problem Set	page 61	page 62	page 63	page 64	page 65	page 66	page 67	page 68	page 69	page 70	page 71	page 72	page 73	page 74	page 75
Logic		X	X	X	X	X	X	X	X							
Critical Thinking										X	X	X	X	X	X	X
Fractions						X	X	X								
Addition/Subtraction Multiplication/Division						X	X	X	X	X	X		X	X	X	X
Measurement															X	
Less Than/Greater Than		X	X									X				
Odd/Even Numbers		X	X	X	X											
Tables										X					X	X
Place Value				X	X											
Money										X				X		

The mystery number is more than 19 but less than 26. What could the number be?

(a) 22   (b) 26   (c) 30   (d) 19

EXTEND THE THINKING: Which other numbers could the mystery number be?

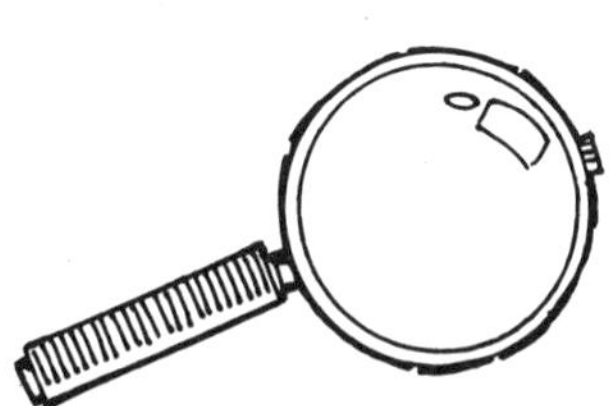

The mystery number is more than 47 but less than 52. What could the number be?

(a) 50   (b) 47   (c) 52   (d) 89

EXTEND THE THINKING: Which other numbers could the mystery number be?

The mystery number is more than 63 but less than 66. It is an odd number. What is the number?

(a) 65   (b) 64   (c) 63   (d) 62

EXTEND THE THINKING: What would the answer be if the mystery number were even?

The mystery number is more than 12 but less than 35. What could the number be?

(a) 26   **(b)** 35   **(c)** 47   **(d)** 10

The mystery number is more than 55 but less than 67. What could the number be?

(a) 59   **(b)** 67   **(c)** 55   **(d)** 34

The mystery number is more than 37 but less than 40. It is an even number. What is the number?

(a) 39   **(b)** 38   **(c)** 37   **(d)** 42

**The mystery number is odd. It has nine tens.
What could the number be?**

   (a) 239　　　　**(b)** 637　　　　**(c)** 930　　　　**(d)** 191

**The mystery number is even. It has six ones.
What could the number be?**

   (a) 376　　　　**(b)** 567　　　　**(c)** 462　　　　**(d)** 839

**The mystery number is even. It has two ones and nine tens.
What could the number be?**

   (a) 792　　　　**(b)** 259　　　　**(c)** 294　　　　**(d)** 329

**The mystery number is even. It has eight tens.
What could the number be?**

(a) 288   **(b)** 681   **(c)** 963   **(d)** 187

**The mystery number is odd. It has nine ones.
What could the number be?**

(a) 379   **(b)** 597   **(c)** 100   **(d)** 842

**The mystery number is odd. It has five hundreds
and seven tens. What could the number be?**

(a) 574   **(b)** 577   **(c)** 578   **(d)** 572

**The number 12 went in and the number 24 came out.
What did the Magic Number Machine do?**

ⓐ doubled ⠀⠀⠀ **ⓑ** cut in half ⠀⠀⠀ **ⓒ** tripled ⠀⠀⠀ **ⓓ** added 10

EXTEND THE THINKING: Write a number sentence that shows how you solved the problem.

**The number 6 went in and the number 18 came out.
What did the Magic Number Machine do?**

ⓐ doubled ⠀⠀⠀ **ⓑ** cut in half ⠀⠀⠀ **ⓒ** tripled ⠀⠀⠀ **ⓓ** added 10

EXTEND THE THINKING: Write a number sentence that shows how you solved the problem.

**The number 68 went in and the number 34 came out.
What did the Magic Number Machine do?**

ⓐ doubled ⠀⠀⠀ **ⓑ** cut in half ⠀⠀⠀ **ⓒ** tripled ⠀⠀⠀ **ⓓ** added 10

EXTEND THE THINKING: Write a number sentence that shows how you solved the problem.

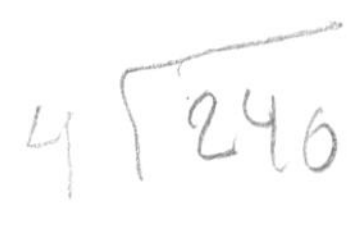

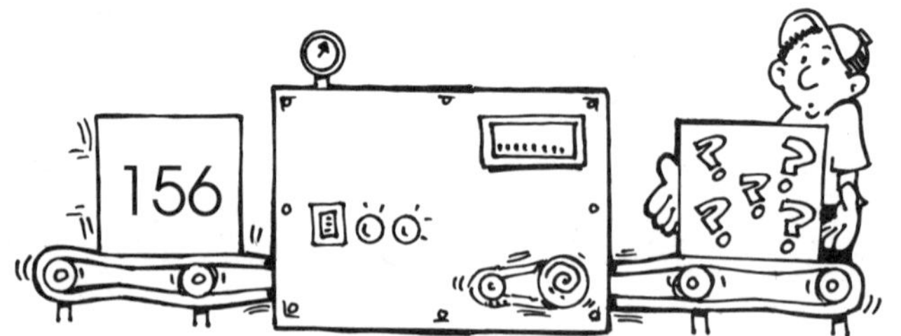

The Magic Number Machine takes 9 away from every number that goes in. If 156 goes in, which number comes out?

(a) 147   (b) 165   (c) 146   (d) 166

EXTEND THE THINKING: Which number would come out if 198 went in?

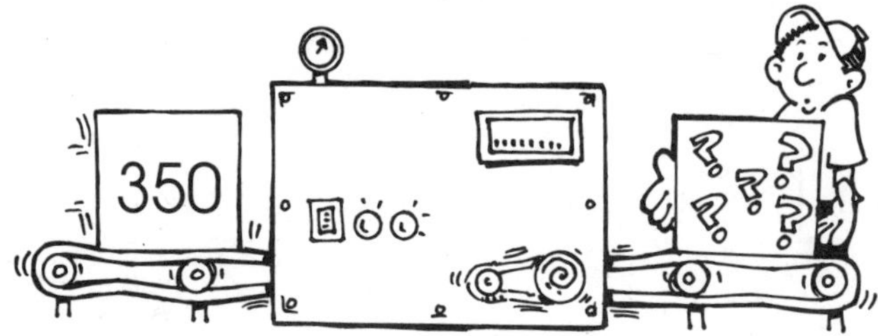

The Magic Number Machine divides in half every number that goes in. If 350 goes in, which number comes out?

(a) 100   (b) 150   (c) 175   (d) 80

EXTEND THE THINKING: Which number would come out if 442 went in?

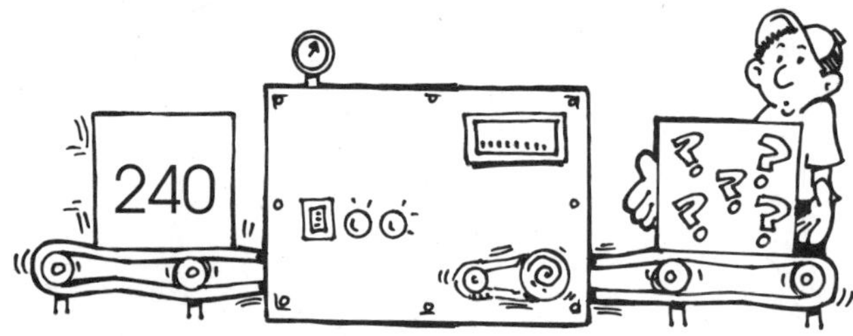

The Magic Number Machine divides into fourths every number that goes in. If 240 goes in, which number comes out?

(a) 480   (b) 160   (c) 60   (d) 120

EXTEND THE THINKING: Which number would come out if 400 went in?

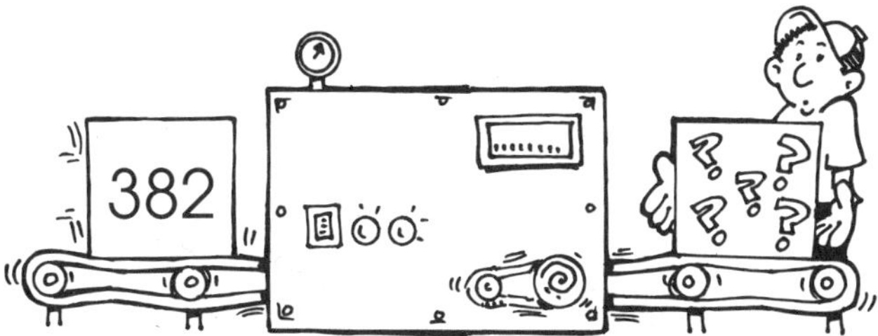

The Magic Number Machine takes 12 away from every number that goes in. If 382 goes in, which number comes out?

(a) 370   (b) 372   (c) 394   (d) 923

EXTEND THE THINKING: Which number would come out if 298 went in?

The Magic Number Machine divides in half every number that goes in. If 268 goes in, which number comes out?

(a) 150   (b) 132   (c) 224   (d) 134

EXTEND THE THINKING: Which number would come out if 654 went in?

The Magic Number Machine divides into thirds every number that goes in. If 270 goes in, which number comes out?

(a) 300   (b) 360   (c) 90   (d) 39

EXTEND THE THINKING: Which number would come out if 336 went in?

Stickers Bought

Hannah	Grace
27	43

If Sue bought twice as many stickers as Hannah, how many stickers did Sue buy?

(a) 27　　　(b) 86　　　(c) 43　　　(d) 54

EXTEND THE THINKING: How many stickers do they have altogether?

Stickers Bought

Hannah	Grace
35	68

If Sue bought half as many stickers as Grace, how many stickers did Sue buy?

(a) 34　　　(b) 68　　　(c) 17　　　(d) 54

EXTEND THE THINKING: Who has more stickers, Hannah or Sue?

Stickers Bought

Hannah	Grace
35	68

If Sue bought three times as many stickers as Hannah, how many stickers did Sue buy?

(a) 105　　　(b) 70　　　(c) 35　　　(d) 54

EXTEND THE THINKING: Write a number sentence that shows how you solved the problem.

Juan has three quarters. Maria has four dimes. Kim has 85 pennies. Who has the greatest amount of money?

ⓐ Carlos   ⓑ Juan   ⓒ Maria   ⓓ Kim

EXTEND THE THINKING: Who has the least amount of money?

Juan has two quarters. Maria has two dimes. Kim has 45 pennies. A toy cat costs 47¢. Who has enough money to buy the toy?

ⓐ Carlos   ⓑ Juan   ⓒ Maria   ⓓ Kim

EXTEND THE THINKING: Write a number sentence that shows how you solved the problem.

Juan has three quarters. Maria has four dimes. Kim has 25 pennies. Which students can combine their money to have exactly one dollar?

ⓐ Carlos and Juan

ⓑ Juan and Kim

ⓒ Maria and Juan

ⓓ Kim and Maria

EXTEND THE THINKING: Write a number sentence that shows how much money the students have altogether.

Casey rode her horse along a trail for 5.5 miles.
Then she turned and rode 4.3 miles.
How many miles did she travel?

ⓐ 98 miles   **ⓑ** 20.8 miles   **ⓒ** 9.8 miles   **ⓓ** 1.2 miles

EXTEND THE THINKING: Write a number sentence that shows how you solved the problem.

Brandon rode his horse along a trail for 5.8 miles.
Then he turned and rode 3.3 miles.
How many miles did he travel?

ⓐ 9.1 miles   **ⓑ** 2.5 miles   **ⓒ** 5.2 miles   **ⓓ** 8.5 miles

EXTEND THE THINKING: Write a number sentence that shows how you solved the problem.

Anna rode her horse along a trail for 6.2 miles.
Then she turned and rode 4.9 miles.
How many miles did she travel?

ⓐ 13.6 miles   **ⓑ** 2.7 miles   **ⓒ** 10.1 miles   **ⓓ** 11.1 miles

EXTEND THE THINKING: Write a number sentence that shows how you solved the problem.

23 • • • 36 • • • • • • ○ • • • • • 54

Which number is probably missing?

(a) 45   (b) 37   (c) 55   (d) 25

a

23 • • • 36 ○ • • • • • • • • • 54

Which number is probably missing?

(a) 45   (b) 37   (c) 55   (d) 25

b

23 • • • 36 • • • • • • • ○ • 54

Which number is probably missing?

(a) 40   (b) 37   (c) 52   (d) 25

c

Which number when added to itself equals 100?

(a) 10 **(b)** 25 **(c)** 50 **(d)** 16

EXTEND THE THINKING: Write a number sentence that shows how you solved the problem.

Which number when added to itself equals 86?

(a) 86 **(b)** 68 **(c)** 43 **(d)** 17

EXTEND THE THINKING: Explain how you solved the problem.

Which number when tripled equals 75?

(a) 15 **(b)** 35 **(c)** 40 **(d)** 25

EXTEND THE THINKING: Explain how you solved the problem.

You can not see the money in your pocket. You know that you have 38¢. Which coin combination is not possible?

(a) 1 quarter, 1 dime, and 3 pennies

(b) 3 dimes and 8 pennies

(c) 3 dimes and 8 nickels

(d) 38 pennies

You can not see the money in your pocket. You know that you have 64¢. Which coin combination is not possible?

(a) 12 dimes

(b) 12 nickels and 4 pennies

(c) 6 dimes and 4 pennies

(d) 10 nickels, 1 dime, and 4 pennies

You can not see the money in your pocket. You know that you have 79¢. Which coin combination is not possible?

(a) 3 quarters and 4 pennies

(b) 6 dimes and 9 pennies

(c) 7 dimes and 9 pennies

(d) 15 nickels and 4 pennies

SPAGHETTI Serves 4
2 cups spaghetti noodles
1 cup meat
2 tablespoons parmesan cheese
2 cups spaghetti sauce

How many cups of meat do you need to serve eight people?

a 3 cups   **b** 6 cups   **c** 4 cups   **d** 2 cups

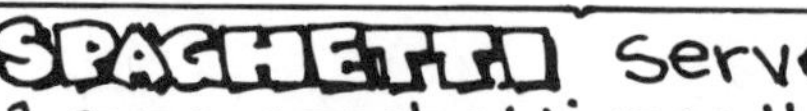

EXTEND THE THINKING: Explain how you solved the problem.

SPAGHETTI Serves 4
2 cups spaghetti noodles
1 cup meat
2 tablespoons parmesan cheese
2 cups spaghetti sauce

If you have six cups of spaghetti sauce, how many people can you serve?

a 13   **b** 6   **c** 14   **d** 12

EXTEND THE THINKING: Explain how you solved the problem.

SPAGHETTI Serves 4
2 cups spaghetti noodles
1 cup meat
2 tablespoons parmesan cheese
2 cups spaghetti sauce

If you want to serve only two people, how much meat do you need?

a 1 cup   **b** $\frac{1}{2}$ cup   **c** $1\frac{1}{2}$ cups   **d** 2 cups

EXTEND THE THINKING: Explain how you solved the problem.

Vowel Code

a = 3 points   e = 6 points
i = 4 points   o = 7 points
u = 5 points

Use the vowel code to find the value of the word *college*.

(a) 19   **(b)** 13   **(c)** 15   **(d)** 20

Vowel Code

a = 3 points   e = 6 points
i = 4 points   o = 7 points
u = 5 points

Use the vowel code to find the value of the word *graduate*.

(a) 20   **(b)** 19   **(c)** 15   **(d)** 17

Vowel Code

a = 3 points   e = 6 points
i = 4 points   o = 7 points
u = 5 points

Use the vowel code to find the word with the greatest value.

(a) rabbit   **(b)** kitten   **(c)** puppy   **(d)** iguana

Section Answers
Logic and Critical Thinking

Correct answers are shaded.

	page 61	page 62	page 63	page 64	page 65
○	**a** b c d	**a** b c d	a b c **d**	**a** b c d	**a** b c d
△	**a** b c d	**a** b c d	**a** b c d	**a** b c d	a b **c** d
□	**a** b c d	a **b** c d	**a** b c d	a **b** c d	a **b** c d

	page 66	page 67	page 68	page 69	page 70
○	**a** b c d	**a** b c d	a b c **d**	a b c **d**	a b **c** d
△	a b **c** d	a b c **d**	**a** b c d	a **b** c d	**a** b c d
□	a b **c** d	a b **c** d	**a** b c d	a **b** c d	a b c **d**

	page 71	page 72	page 73	page 74	page 75
○	**a** b c d	a b **c** d	a b **c** d	a b c **d**	**a** b c d
△	a **b** c d	a b **c** d	**a** b c d	a b c **d**	a b c **d**
□	a b **c** d	a b c **d**	a **b** c d	a **b** c d	a b c **d**

Measurement

The *Level D* Measurement standards require students to

- tell time and identify a time before and after a given time
- estimate standard measurements (e.g., inches)
- read a thermometer
- compare size, weight, height, and capacity
- apply concepts of measurement to real life
- identify and calculate money

Classroom Store

Put toy and clothing catalogs, advertisement inserts, and play money at a learning center. Invite students to make a wish list of items they'd like to buy, including the price. Have students work with a budget (e.g., $15.00) and add and subtract items to stay within their budget. Have students "buy" large quantities of an item to practice multiplication (e.g., *If you want to buy ten dolls, how much money do you need?*). As an option, give students a weekly "shopping list" of items. Have students search the advertisement inserts to find the best prices. Challenge them to spend the least amount of money to buy everything on their list.

Measurement Tools

Divide the class into teams of four students each. Give each team a measurement tool (e.g., measuring cup, teaspoon, centimeter or inch ruler, scale) and an index card. Encourage each team to use their tool to create a problem. Have them write their problem on the index card for the other students to solve using that measurement tool.

TEST-TAKING TIPS
FOR STUDENTS

- ✔ Eat a good breakfast the morning of a test.
- ✔ Have a healthy snack before the test.
- ✔ Believe in yourself.

TEACHING TIP
FOR THIS SECTION

Tell students that they can sometimes more easily solve a measurement problem by creating a chart to compare the measurements. For example, have students copy the chart in the ● problem on page 82 and fill in the missing measurements. Then, have them use the complete chart to answer the question (a).

→ Answers are on page 94.

Concepts: Measurement

Problem Set	Money	Addition/Subtraction Multiplication/Division	Time	Perimeter	Area	Length/Height/Width	Distance	Weight	Temperature
page 79						X			
page 80						X			
page 81		X						X	
page 82		X					X		
page 83	X	X							
page 84	X	X							
page 85		X	X						
page 86		X	X						
page 87		X	X						
page 88		X							X
page 89		X							X
page 90		X		X					
page 91		X			X				
page 92		X					X		
page 93		X							

Use your ruler to find the length of the rectangle in inches.

(a) 1 inch   (b) 3 inches   (c) 2 inches   (d) $2\frac{1}{2}$ inches

---

Use your ruler to find the length of the rectangle in inches.

(a) 3 inches   (b) $3\frac{1}{2}$ inches   (c) $1\frac{3}{4}$ inches   (d) $2\frac{1}{2}$ inches

---

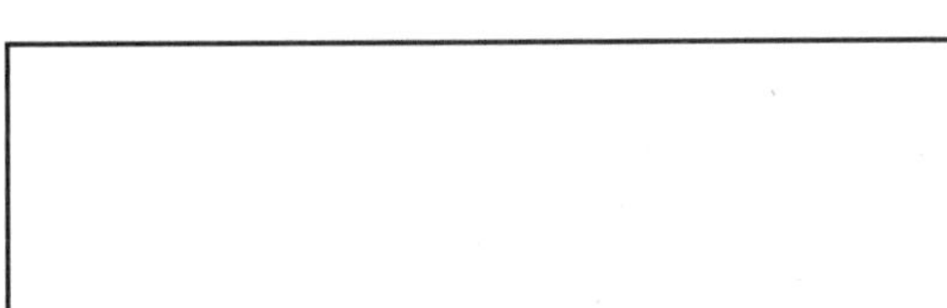

Use your ruler to find the length of the rectangle in inches.

(a) 2 inches   (b) $1\frac{1}{2}$ inches   (c) $1\frac{3}{4}$ inches   (d) $2\frac{3}{4}$ inches

Use your ruler to find the width of the coin in centimeters.

(a) 2 centimeters   **(b)** 3.5 centimeters   **(c)** 3 centimeters   **(d)** 5 centimeters

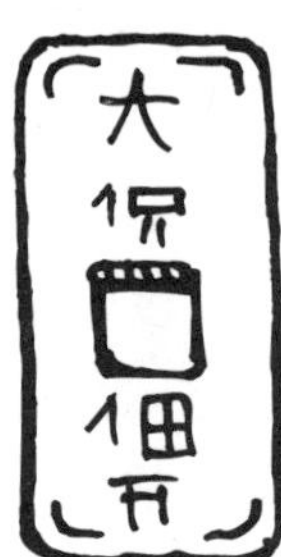

Use your ruler to find the height of the coin in centimeters.

(a) 2 centimeters   **(b)** 2.5 centimeters   **(c)** 5.8 centimeters   **(d)** 3.5 centimeters

Use your ruler to find the width of the coin in centimeters.

(a) 2.2 centimeters   **(b)** 3.3 centimeters   **(c)** 3.8 centimeters   **(d)** 2.5 centimeters

Which puppy weighs the most?

ⓐ Thor **ⓑ** Lady **ⓒ** Bud **ⓓ** Rex

EXTEND THE THINKING: Which puppy weighs the least?

Which puppies are equal in weight?

ⓐ Thor and Rex **ⓑ** Lady and Thor **ⓒ** Bud and Thor **ⓓ** Rex and Bud

EXTEND THE THINKING: Which puppy weighs about seven pounds?

If both Bud and Rex sat together on a scale, their combined weight would equal the weight of which other puppy?

ⓐ Thor **ⓑ** Lady **ⓒ** Bud **ⓓ** Rex

EXTEND THE THINKING: How many kilograms does Thor weigh?

Distance Hopped by a Rabbit

	Centimeters	Meters
Bounce		4
Hoppy	50	
Skippy	350	
Fluff		$3\frac{1}{2}$

Which rabbit hopped the longest distance?

a Bounce   **b** Hoppy   **c** Skippy   **d** Fluff

EXTEND THE THINKING: Which rabbit hopped the shortest distance?

Distance Hopped by a Rabbit

	Centimeters	Meters
Bounce		4
Hoppy	50	
Skippy	350	
Fluff		$3\frac{1}{2}$

Fluff jumped farther than which other rabbit?

a Bounce   **b** Hoppy   **c** Skippy   **d** Fluff

EXTEND THE THINKING: How many centimeters did Bounce jump?

Distance Hopped by a Rabbit

	Centimeters	Meters
Bounce		4
Hoppy	50	
Skippy	350	
Fluff		$3\frac{1}{2}$

Which two rabbits hopped an equal distance?

a Bounce and Hoppy   **b** Hoppy and Fluff   **c** Skippy and Fluff   **d** Fluff and Bounce

EXTEND THE THINKING: How many meters did Bounce and Hoppy jump altogether?

Sam has a $20.00 bill. Which coin does he need to buy the football if it costs $20.25?

(a) 1 dime   (b) 1 nickel   (c) 1 quarter   (d) 1 penny

Sam has a $20.00 bill. Which coins does he need to buy the football if it costs $20.30?

(a) 1 dime and 1 quarter   (b) 1 nickel and 1 quarter   (c) 2 quarters   (d) 2 dimes

Sam has $21.00. Which coin will he receive as change if the football costs $20.75?

(a) 1 dime   (b) 1 nickel   (c) 1 quarter   (d) 1 penny

You have two dimes. Which snack can you buy?

ⓐ pretzel   **ⓑ** popcorn   **ⓒ** chips   **ⓓ** apple

EXTEND THE THINKING: How much money will you have left?

**You have three dimes, one nickel, and two pennies.
Which snack costs more than you can afford?**

ⓐ pretzel   **ⓑ** popcorn   **ⓒ** chips   **ⓓ** apple

EXTEND THE THINKING: How much more money would you need to buy that snack?

**You have two dimes, two nickels, and one penny.
Which snacks can you buy?**

ⓐ 2 pretzels   **ⓑ** 2 apples   **ⓒ** chips and popcorn   **ⓓ** apple and chips

EXTEND THE THINKING: How much money will you have left after buying the snacks?

What time will it be in $2\frac{1}{2}$ hours?

ⓐ 5:00   **ⓑ** 4:00   **ⓒ** 5:30   **ⓓ** 6:00

What time will it be in $4\frac{1}{2}$ hours?

ⓐ 4:45   **ⓑ** 1:30   **ⓒ** 3:15   **ⓓ** 4:00

What time will it be in 6 hours and 15 minutes?

ⓐ 6:15   **ⓑ** 12:45   **ⓒ** 7:45   **ⓓ** 6:45

What time was it a half hour ago?

(a) 9:45 (b) 9:30 (c) 9:15 (d) 9:00

What time was it 15 minutes ago?

(a) 4:00 (b) 4:15 (c) 4:30 (d) 4:45

What time was it 45 minutes ago?

(a) 1:00 (b) 1:15 (c) 12:45 (d) 12:00

Your favorite show starts in a half hour. At what time does it begin?

ⓐ 3:30   **ⓑ** 4:00   **ⓒ** 3:00   **ⓓ** 9:30

Your favorite show starts in 15 minutes. At what time does it begin?

ⓐ 3:00   **ⓑ** 3:15   **ⓒ** 3:30   **ⓓ** 3:45

Your favorite show starts in 15 minutes. At what time does it begin?

ⓐ 4:00   **ⓑ** 3:00   **ⓒ** 3:30   **ⓓ** 3:45

If it becomes 5 degrees warmer,
what will the temperature be?

(a) 85°   **(b)** 80°   **(c)** 90°   **(d)** 75°

EXTEND THE THINKING: If it becomes 10 degrees cooler, what will the temperature be?

If it becomes 5 degrees warmer,
what will the temperature be?

(a) 95°   **(b)** 90°   **(c)** 85°   **(d)** 70°

EXTEND THE THINKING: If it becomes 15 degrees cooler, what will the temperature be?

If it becomes 5 degrees warmer,
what will the temperature be?

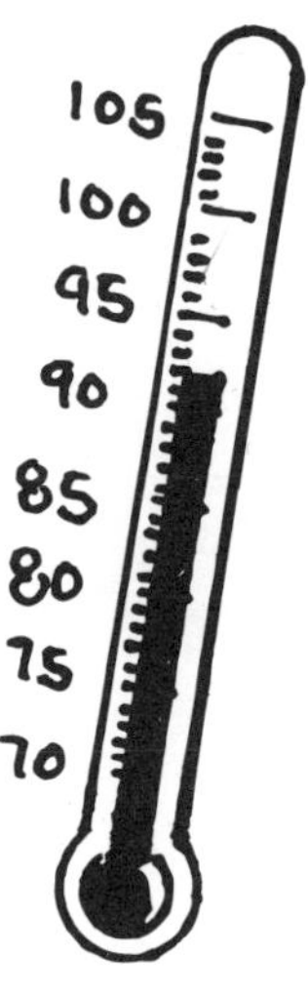

(a) 92°   **(b)** 97°   **(c)** 100°   **(d)** 94°

EXTEND THE THINKING: If it becomes 4 degrees cooler, what will the temperature be?

If it becomes 7 degrees warmer,
what will the temperature be?

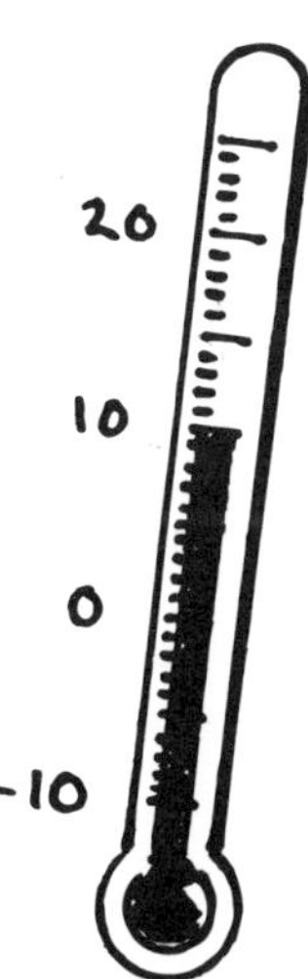

(a) 15°   **(b)** 23°   **(c)** 17°   **(d)** 10°

If it becomes 6 degrees cooler,
what will the temperature be?

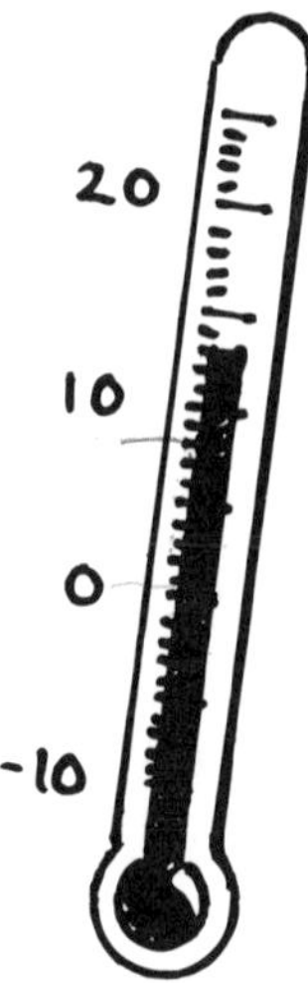

(a) 13°   **(b)** 7°   **(c)** 20°   **(d)** 19°

If it becomes 4 degrees warmer,
what will the temperature be?

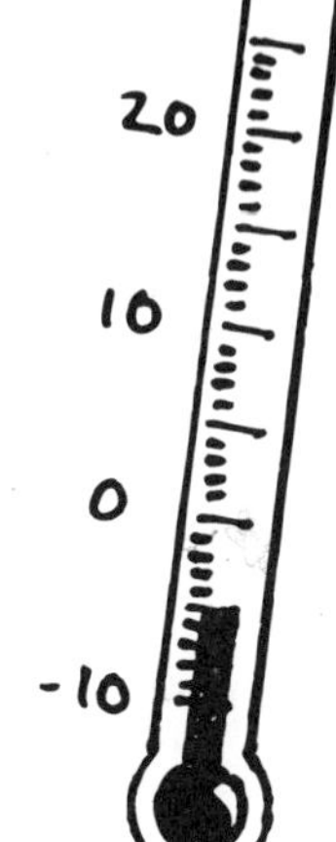

(a) 5°   **(b)** 9°   **(c)** -1°   **(d)** -5°

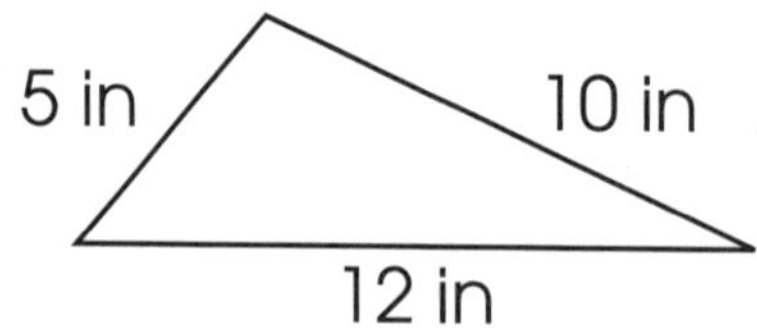

What is the perimeter of the triangle?

ⓐ 12 in   ⓑ 27 in   ⓒ 12 ft   ⓓ 27 ft

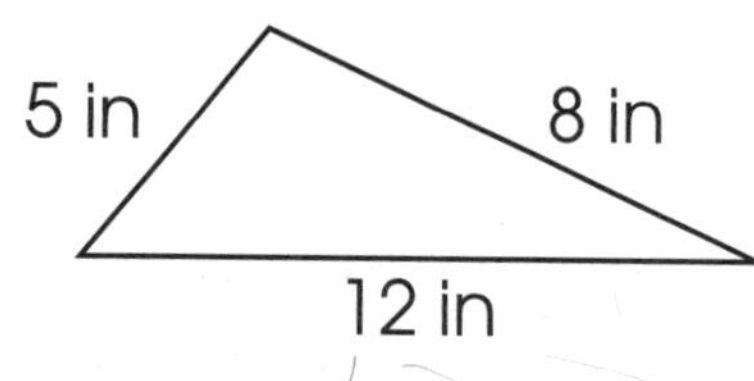

What is the perimeter of the triangle?

ⓐ 25 in   ⓑ 27 in   ⓒ 20 in   ⓓ 17 in

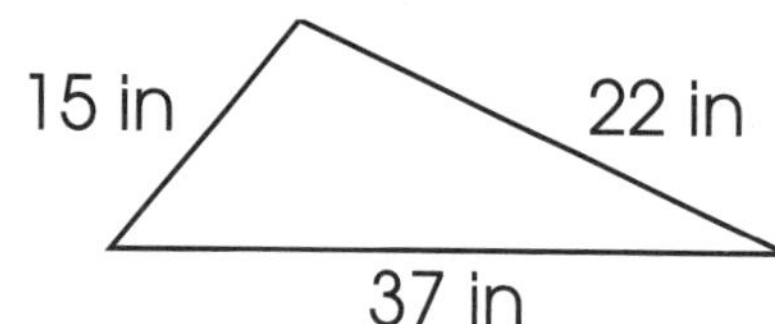

What is the perimeter of the triangle?

ⓐ 74 in   ⓑ 84 in   ⓒ 77 in   ⓓ 72 in

If the area of square A is 16 cm², what do you estimate is the area of rectangle B?

ⓐ 20 cm²   **ⓑ** 10 cm²   **ⓒ** 8 cm²   **ⓓ** 4 cm²

EXTEND THE THINKING: Write a number sentence that shows how you solved the problem.

If the area of square A is 36 cm², what do you estimate is the area of rectangle B?

ⓐ 18 cm²   **ⓑ** 16 cm²   **ⓒ** 6 cm²   **ⓓ** 8 cm²

EXTEND THE THINKING: Write a number sentence that shows how you solved the problem.

If the area of square A is 64 cm², what do you estimate is the area of rectangle B?

ⓐ 32 cm²   **ⓑ** 35 cm²   **ⓒ** 48 cm²   **ⓓ** 16 cm²

EXTEND THE THINKING: Write a number sentence that shows how you solved the problem.

Which town is closest to Rochester?

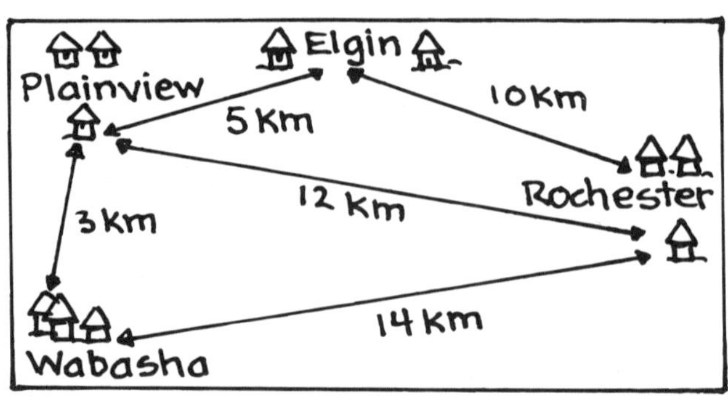

ⓐ Rochester

ⓑ Elgin

ⓒ Plainview

ⓓ Wabasha

EXTEND THE THINKING: Which town is furthest from Rochester?

Plainview is the only town without a grocery store. Where would people in Plainview shop if they wanted the closest store?

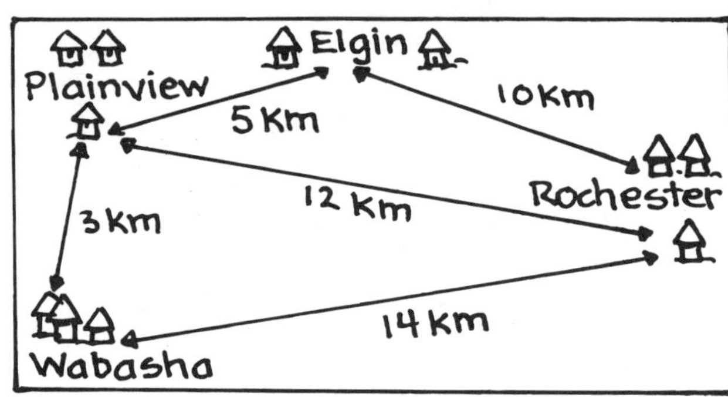

ⓐ Rochester

ⓑ Elgin

ⓒ Plainview

ⓓ Wabasha

EXTEND THE THINKING: Write a number sentence that shows how you solved the problem.

Elgin is 8 km from which town?

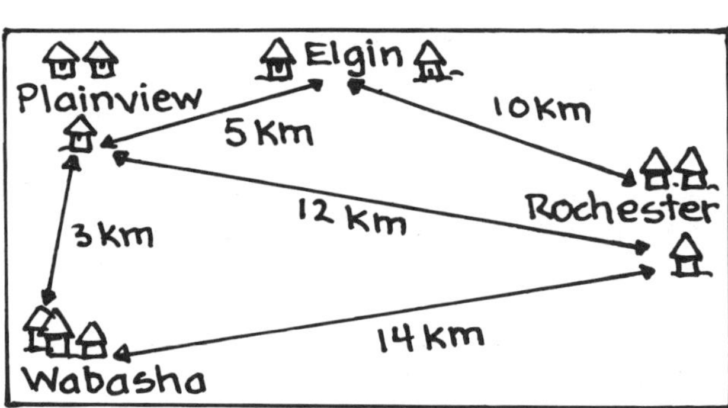

ⓐ Rochester

ⓑ Elgin

ⓒ Plainview

ⓓ Wabasha

EXTEND THE THINKING: Write a number sentence that shows how you solved the problem.

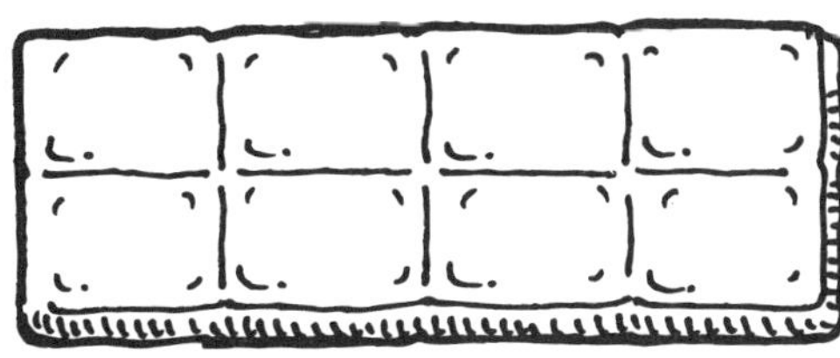

You have a chocolate bar with eight pieces. If you eat four pieces, what fraction have you eaten?

ⓐ $\dfrac{4}{8}$ ⓑ $\dfrac{1}{3}$ ⓒ $\dfrac{4}{10}$ ⓓ $\dfrac{4}{5}$

EXTEND THE THINKING: Explain how you solved the problem.

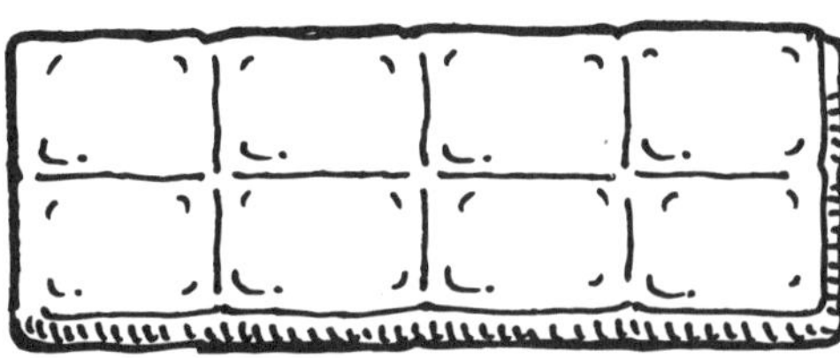

You have a chocolate bar with eight pieces. If you eat two pieces, what fraction have you eaten?

ⓐ $\dfrac{1}{4}$ ⓑ $\dfrac{1}{3}$ ⓒ $\dfrac{1}{2}$ ⓓ $\dfrac{1}{8}$

EXTEND THE THINKING: How many pieces will you have left?

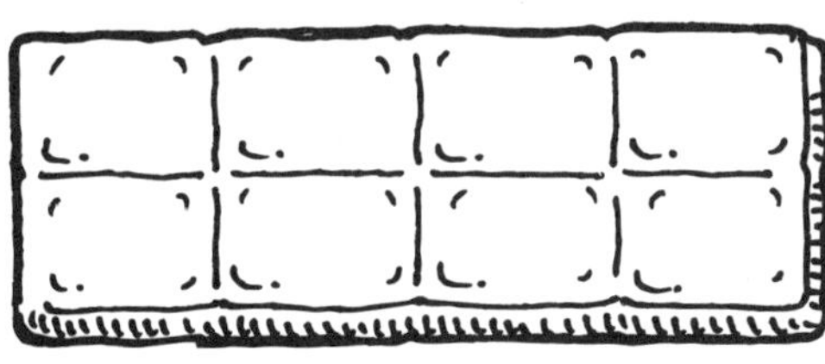

You have a chocolate bar with eight pieces. If you eat one eighth of the bar, how many pieces have you eaten?

ⓐ 8 ⓑ 2 ⓒ 4 ⓓ 1

EXTEND THE THINKING: Explain how you solved the problem.

Section Answers
Measurement

Correct answers are shaded.

	page 79	page 80	page 81	page 82	page 83
○	a **b** c d	**a** b c d	a **b** c d	**a** b c d	a b **c** d
△	a **b** c d	a b c **d**	a b c **d**	a **b** c d	a **b** c d
▢	a b c **d**	a b c **d**	a **b** c d	a b **c** d	a b **c** d

	page 84	page 85	page 86	page 87	page 88
○	**a** b c d	a b c **d**	a b **c** d	a **b** c d	**a** b c d
△	a b c **d**	**a** b c d	a **b** c d	a b **c** d	**a** b c d
▢	**a** b c d	a **b** c d	a b c **d**	**a** b c d	a **b** c d

	page 89	page 90	page 91	page 92	page 93
○	a b **c** d	a **b** c d	a b **c** d	a **b** c d	**a** b c d
△	a **b** c d	**a** b c d	**a** b c d	a b c **d**	**a** b c d
▢	a b **c** d	**a** b c d	**a** b c d	a b c **d**	a b c **d**

Mathematical Reasoning

The *Level D* Mathematical Reasoning standards require students to

- use discrete math—determine the total number of different ways in which shapes, objects, and numbers can be arranged

- use analogies—compare and contrast shapes, solids, or numbers; examine attributes; and apply basic math concepts to discover the relationship between geometric and numerical pairs

- use problem-solving skills—apply basic math concepts to real-life situations

Discrete Caps

Cut out for each student 16 small oval hats from four different colors of construction paper (e.g., four blue, four green, four red, four yellow). Give each student a set of hats and a piece of white construction paper. Have students fold the construction paper in half twice in each direction to make 16 boxes. Read aloud *Caps for Sale* by Esphyr Slobodkina (HarperTrophy). Ask students to determine all the possible ways the monkeys could wear the hats. Remind them that a monkey can only wear one hat of each color at a time. Have students manipulate the hats to figure out the problem.

Analogy Cards

Give each student an index card. Have students divide it in half by folding it and drawing a line down the middle. Invite each student to write an analogy on the card and then cover up the answer with a sticky note. Have students trade cards and solve each other's analogy.

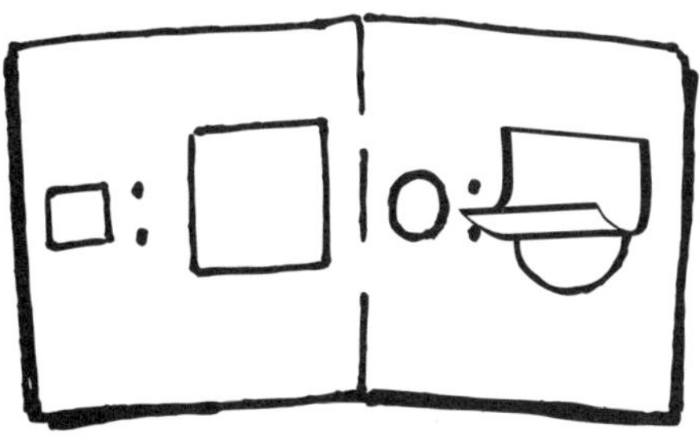

Concepts: Mathematical Reasoning

Math Concept	Problem Set	page 97	page 98	page 99	page 100	page 101	page 102	page 103	page 104	page 105	page 106	page 107	page 108	page 109	page 110	page 111
Discrete Math		X	X	X												
Analogies					X	X	X	X								
Problem Solving									X	X	X	X	X	X	X	X
Volume															X	
Shapes/Solids					X	X										
Tables									X	X						
Greater Than/Less Than											X	X				
Addition/Subtraction Multiplication/Division							X	X	X	X	X		X	X		
Pie Graphs													X	X		
Fractions															X	X

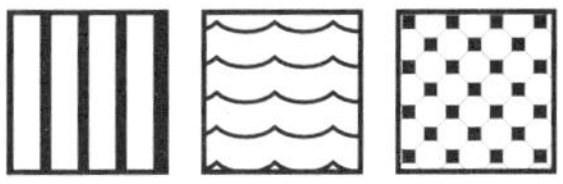

These three cards are shuffled and placed facedown on a table. You choose one card at a time. In which order could you choose the cards?

a 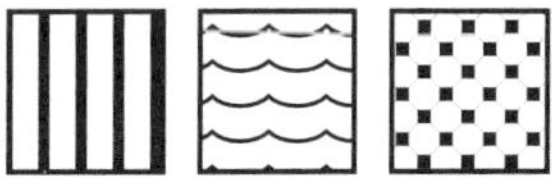

b 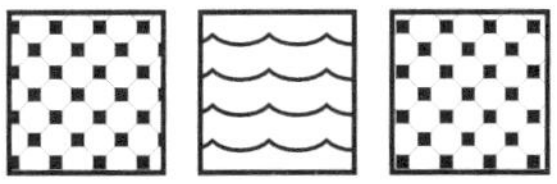

c 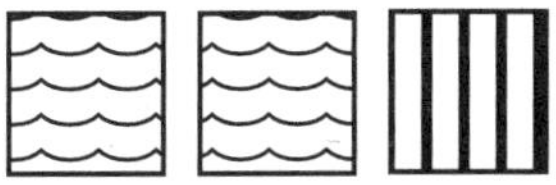

d 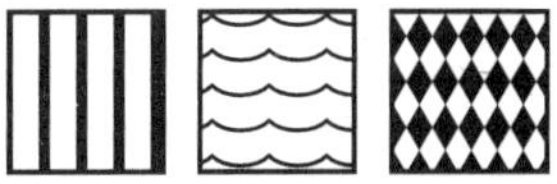

EXTEND THE THINKING: In which other orders could you choose the cards?

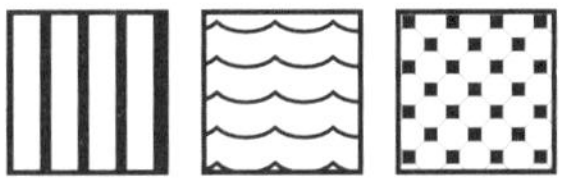

These three cards are shuffled and placed facedown on a table. You choose one card at a time. In which order could you not choose the cards?

a 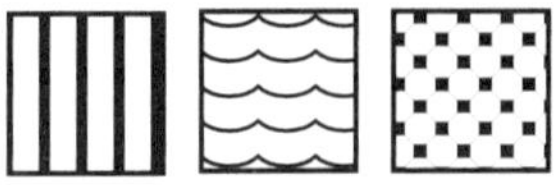

b 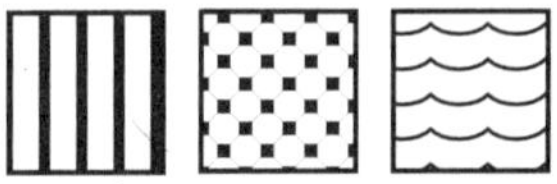

c 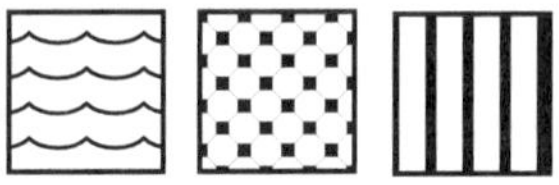

d 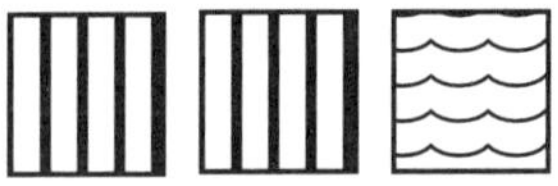

EXTEND THE THINKING: In which other orders could you choose the cards?

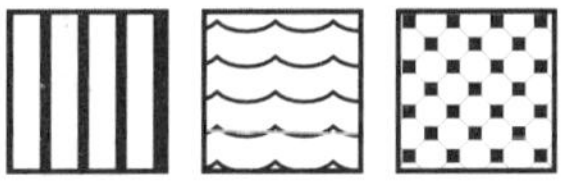

These three cards are shuffled and placed facedown on a table. You pick the 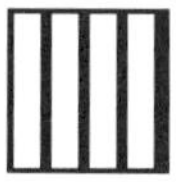 card first. In which order could you choose the cards?

a 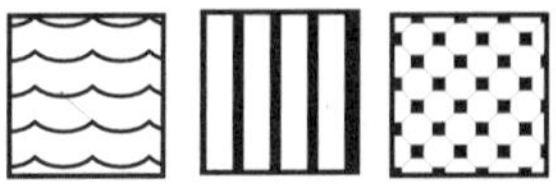

b 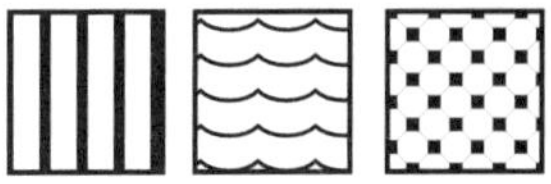

c 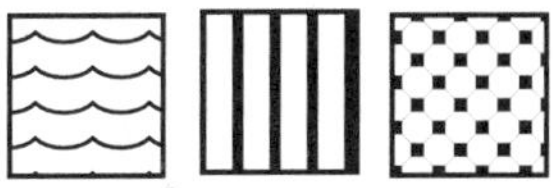

d 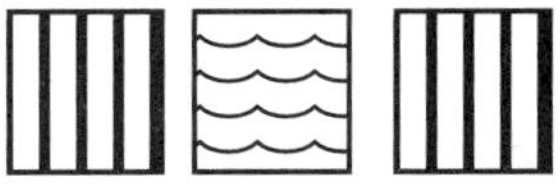

EXTEND THE THINKING: In which other orders could you choose the cards?

There are three toys in a piñata: one pencil, one eraser, and one small ball. In which order could they fall out of the piñata?

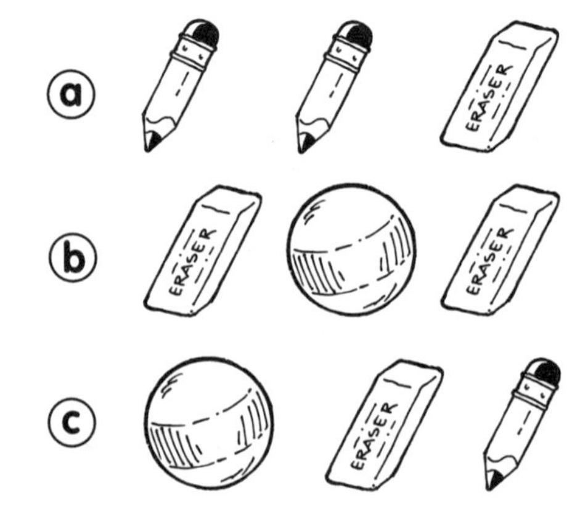

ⓐ

ⓑ

ⓒ

ⓓ

There are three toys in a piñata: one pencil, one eraser, and one small ball. In which order could they not fall out of the piñata?

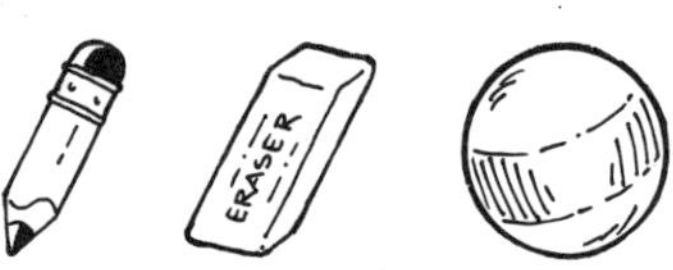

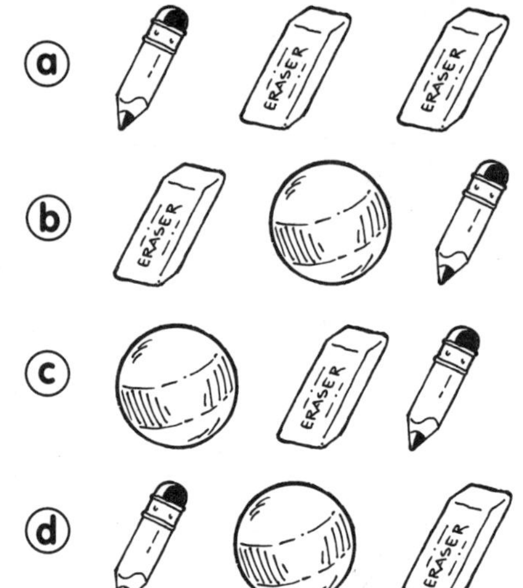

ⓐ

ⓑ

ⓒ

ⓓ

There are three toys in a piñata: one pencil, one eraser, and one small ball. In which order could they not fall out of the piñata?

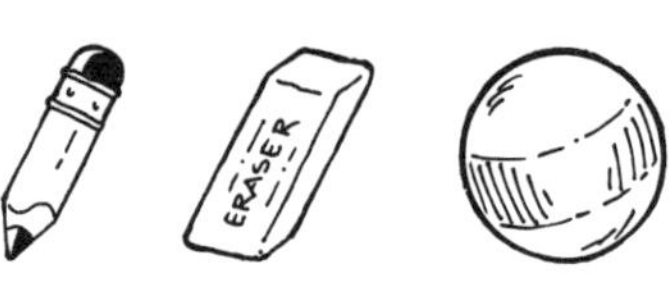

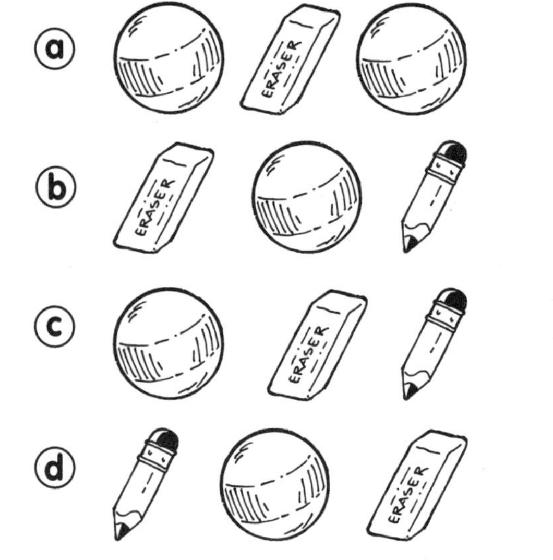

ⓐ

ⓑ

ⓒ

ⓓ

You have a cupcake and one red, one blue, and one green candle. In how many different ways can you line up the candles on the cupcake?

(a) 4   (b) 3   (c) 6   (d) 10

EXTEND THE THINKING: Draw one possible order of the candles.

You have a cupcake and one red, one blue, and one green candle. In which way is it possible to line up the candles on the cupcake?

(a) red, blue, green

(b) blue, green, blue

(c) red, blue, blue

(d) green, red, green

EXTEND THE THINKING: Which other arrangements are possible?

You have a cupcake and one red, one blue, and one green candle. In which way is it not possible to line up the candles on the cupcake?

(a) red, blue, green

(b) red, green, blue

(c) red, blue, blue

(d) blue, red, green

EXTEND THE THINKING: Which other arrangements are possible?

● : ◯ as ■ : ___

a ●   b ◯   c ■   d ▢

EXTEND THE THINKING: Explain how you solved the problem.

▢ : ⊠ as ◐ : ___

a ◐   b ⊗   c ▱   d ⊕

EXTEND THE THINKING: Explain how you solved the problem.

◯ : ○ as △ : ___

a ▢   b △   c ○   d △

EXTEND THE THINKING: Explain how you solved the problem.

: as : _______

(a) (b) (c) (d)

: as : _______

(a) (b) (c) (d)

: 4 as : _______

(a) 5 (b) 6 (c) 7 (d) 8

$$4 : 40 \text{ as } 5 : \underline{\quad}$$

(a) 15   **(b)** 50   **(c)** 55   **(d)** 45

EXTEND THE THINKING: Explain how you solved the problem.

$$3 : 33 \text{ as } 7 : \underline{\quad}$$

(a) 33   **(b)** 66   **(c)** 88   **(d)** 77

EXTEND THE THINKING: Explain how you solved the problem.

$$5 : 55 \text{ as } 7 : \underline{\quad}$$

(a) 75   **(b)** 78   **(c)** 67   **(d)** 57

EXTEND THE THINKING: Explain how you solved the problem.

$$3 : 6 \text{ as } 9 : \rule{2em}{0.4pt}$$

(a) 11   (b) 18   (c) 24   (d) 2

$$3 : 15 \text{ as } 5 : \rule{2em}{0.4pt}$$

(a) 11   (b) 15   (c) 25   (d) 20

$$4 : 16 \text{ as } 6 : \rule{2em}{0.4pt}$$

(a) 42   (b) 20   (c) 36   (d) 17

How many miles is it from Rochester to Bemidji?

To	Albert Leah	Austin	Bemidji	Fergus Falls	Minneapolis
From					
Duluth	251	255	153	211	157
Rochester	64	36	315	277	94
St. Cloud	165	169	150	120	72

ⓐ 64 miles   **ⓑ** 277 miles   **ⓒ** 315 miles   **ⓓ** 153 miles

EXTEND THE THINKING: How many miles is it from Rochester to Fergus Falls?

Which city is furthest from Duluth?

To	Albert Leah	Austin	Bemidji	Fergus Falls	Minneapolis
From					
Duluth	251	255	153	211	157
Rochester	64	36	315	277	94
St. Cloud	165	169	150	120	72

ⓐ Albert Leah   **ⓑ** Austin   **ⓒ** Bemidji   **ⓓ** Fergus Falls

EXTEND THE THINKING: Which cities are closer to St. Cloud than Albert Leah or Austin?

How many more miles is it from Rochester to Bemidji than from Duluth to Minneapolis?

To	Albert Leah	Austin	Bemidji	Fergus Falls	Minneapolis
From					
Duluth	251	255	153	211	157
Rochester	64	36	315	277	94
St. Cloud	165	169	150	120	72

ⓐ 315 miles   **ⓑ** 158 miles   **ⓒ** 157 miles   **ⓓ** 472 miles

EXTEND THE THINKING: If you start in Austin, will it take longer to drive to Duluth or St. Cloud?

How many miles is it from San Diego to San Francisco?

To	Fresno	Sacramento	San Francisco	San Luis Obispo
From				
Monterey	158	186	115	143
Palm Springs	328	499	493	309
Riverside	274	445	439	251
San Diego	339	510	504	319

ⓐ 339 miles **ⓑ** 510 miles **ⓒ** 504 miles **ⓓ** 319 miles

EXTEND THE THINKING: How many miles is it from San Diego to San Luis Obispo?

Which city is furthest from Monterey?

To	Fresno	Sacramento	San Francisco	San Luis Obispo
From				
Monterey	158	186	115	143
Palm Springs	328	499	493	309
Riverside	274	445	439	251
San Diego	339	510	504	319

ⓐ Sacramento **ⓑ** San Francisco **ⓒ** Fresno **ⓓ** San Luis Obispo

EXTEND THE THINKING: Explain how you solved the problem.

How many more miles is it from San Diego to San Francisco than from Palm Springs to San Francisco?

To	Fresno	Sacramento	San Francisco	San Luis Obispo
From				
Monterey	158	186	115	143
Palm Springs	328	499	493	309
Riverside	274	445	439	251
San Diego	339	510	504	319

ⓐ 11 miles **ⓑ** 9 miles **ⓒ** 504 miles **ⓓ** 1 mile

EXTEND THE THINKING: Explain how you solved the problem.

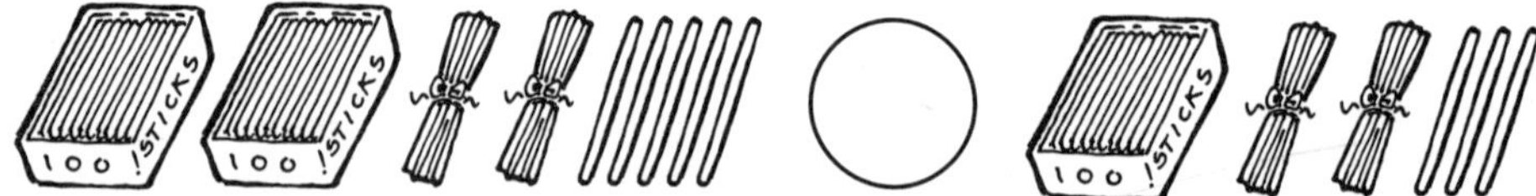

There are 100 sticks in a box and ten sticks in a bundle. Which symbol completes the number sentence?

   (a) >   (b) <   (c) =   (d) +

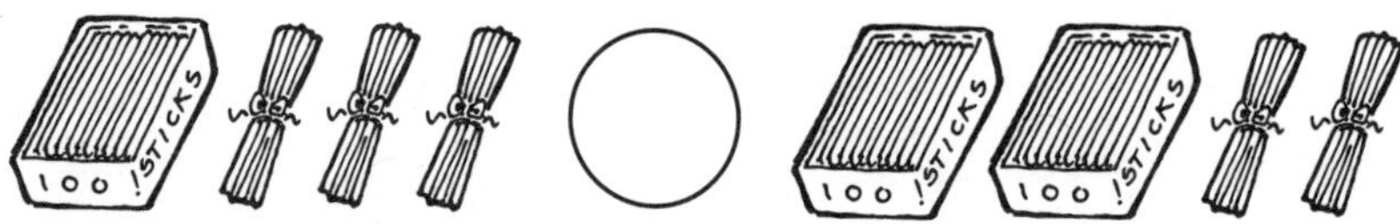

There are 100 sticks in a box and ten sticks in a bundle. Which symbol completes the number sentence?

   (a) >   (b) <   (c) =   (d) +

There are 100 sticks in a box and ten sticks in a bundle. Which symbol completes the number sentence?

   (a) >   (b) <   (c) =   (d) +

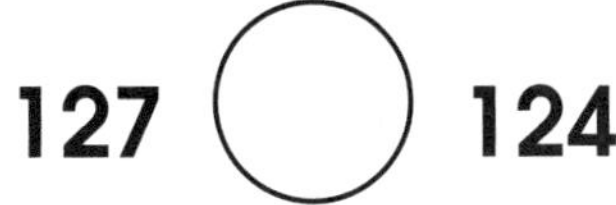

127 ◯ 124

Which symbol completes the number sentence?

ⓐ >   ⓑ <   ⓒ =   ⓓ +

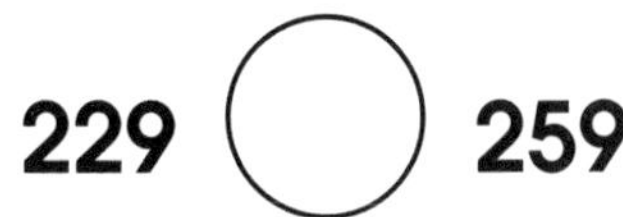

229 ◯ 259

Which symbol completes the number sentence?

ⓐ >   ⓑ <   ⓒ =   ⓓ +

449 ◯ 649

Which symbol completes the number sentence?

ⓐ >   ⓑ <   ⓒ =   ⓓ +

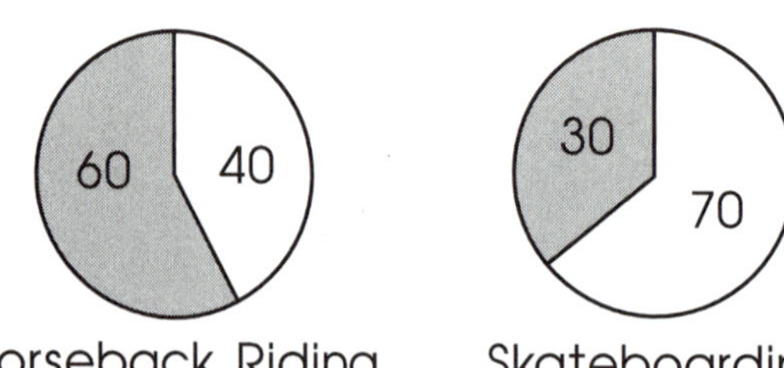

Which group is more likely to participate in horseback riding?

(a) girls   **(b)** boys   **(c)** neither

EXTEND THE THINKING: Is the same group more likely to participate in skateboarding?

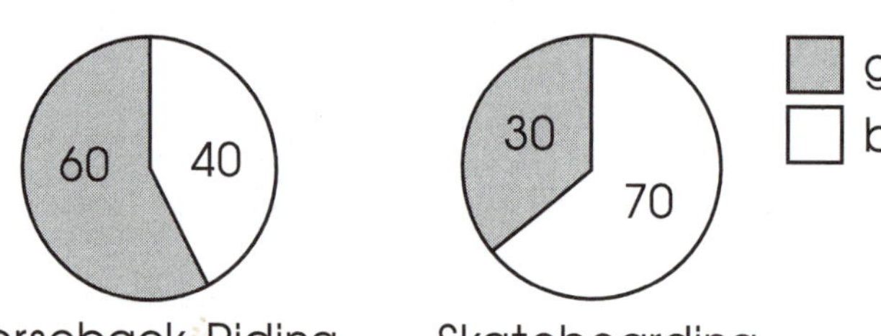

Which group is more likely to participate in skateboarding?

(a) girls   **(b)** boys   **(c)** neither

EXTEND THE THINKING: Are girls more likely to participate in horseback riding or skateboarding?

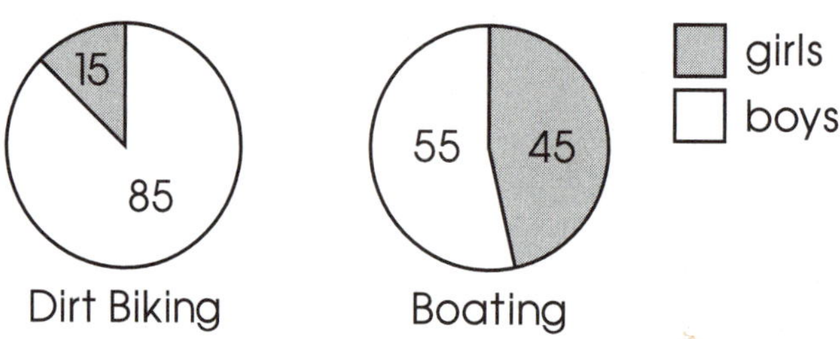

Are girls more likely to participate in dirt biking or boating?

(a) dirt biking   **(b)** boating   **(c)** neither

EXTEND THE THINKING: Are boys more likely to participate in dirt biking or boating?

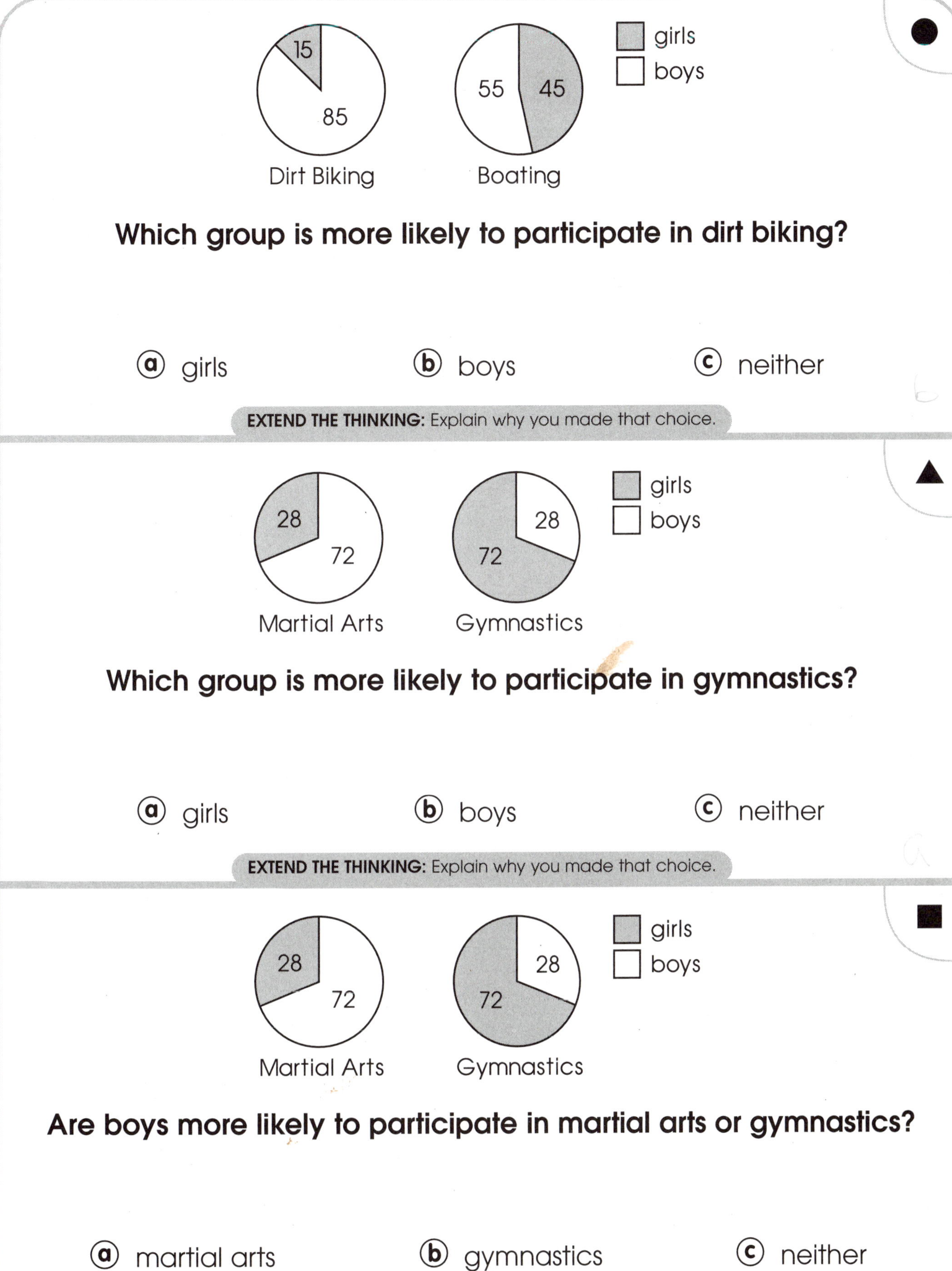

Which group is more likely to participate in dirt biking?

a girls   **b** boys   **c** neither

EXTEND THE THINKING: Explain why you made that choice.

Which group is more likely to participate in gymnastics?

a girls   **b** boys   **c** neither

EXTEND THE THINKING: Explain why you made that choice.

Are boys more likely to participate in martial arts or gymnastics?

a martial arts   **b** gymnastics   **c** neither

EXTEND THE THINKING: What percentage of girls participate in martial arts?

What is the order of cups from smallest to largest?

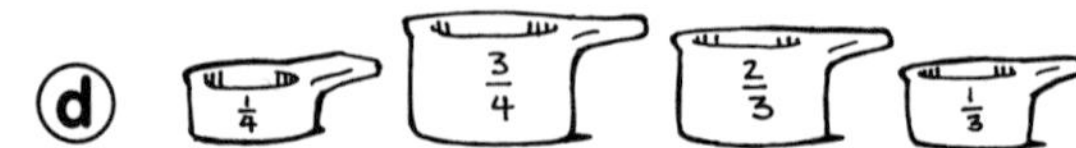

What is the order of spoons from smallest to largest?

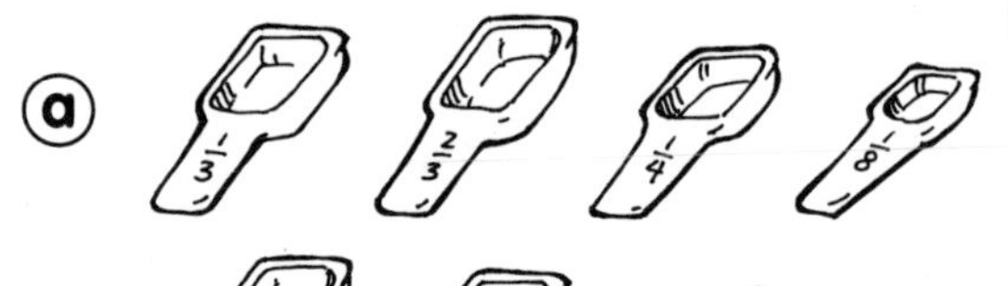

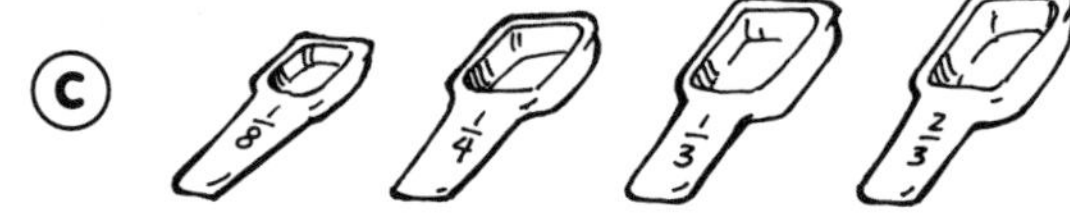

What is the order of cups from smallest to largest?

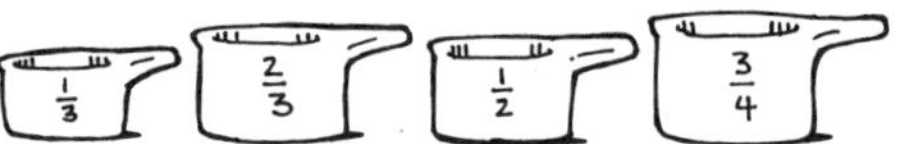

What is the order of fractions from smallest to largest?

(a) $\dfrac{1}{4}, \dfrac{3}{4}, \dfrac{2}{3}, \dfrac{1}{3}$ (b) $\dfrac{1}{3}, \dfrac{2}{3}, \dfrac{1}{4}, \dfrac{3}{4}$ (c) $\dfrac{2}{3}, \dfrac{1}{3}, \dfrac{2}{3}, \dfrac{3}{4}$ (d) $\dfrac{1}{4}, \dfrac{1}{3}, \dfrac{2}{3}, \dfrac{3}{4}$

EXTEND THE THINKING: Name a fraction that is larger than any of these fractions.

What is the order of fractions from largest to smallest?

(a) $\dfrac{1}{8}, \dfrac{1}{4}, \dfrac{1}{3}, \dfrac{2}{3}$ (b) $\dfrac{2}{3}, \dfrac{1}{3}, \dfrac{1}{4}, \dfrac{1}{8}$ (c) $\dfrac{1}{4}, \dfrac{1}{3}, \dfrac{2}{3}, \dfrac{1}{8}$ (d) $\dfrac{1}{3}, \dfrac{2}{3}, \dfrac{1}{4}, \dfrac{1}{8}$

EXTEND THE THINKING: What is the order of fractions from smallest to largest?

What is the order of fractions from largest to smallest?

(a) $\dfrac{3}{4}, \dfrac{2}{3}, \dfrac{1}{2}, \dfrac{1}{3}$ (b) $\dfrac{1}{2}, \dfrac{1}{3}, \dfrac{2}{3}, \dfrac{3}{4}$ (c) $\dfrac{3}{4}, \dfrac{1}{2}, \dfrac{2}{3}, \dfrac{1}{3}$ (d) $\dfrac{3}{4}, \dfrac{2}{3}, \dfrac{1}{3}, \dfrac{1}{2}$

EXTEND THE THINKING: What is twice the smallest fraction?

Section Answers
Mathematical Reasoning

Correct answers are shaded.

	page 97	page 98	page 99	page 100	page 101
○	**a** b c d	a b **c** d	a b **c** d	a b c **d**	a b c **d**
△	a b c **d**	**a** b c d	**a** b c d	a b c **d**	**a** b c d
□	a **b** c d	**a** b c d	a b **c** d	a **b** c d	**a** b c d

	page 102	page 103	page 104	page 105	page 106
○	a **b** c d	a **b** c d	a b **c** d	a b **c** d	**a** b c d
△	a b c **d**	a b **c** d	a **b** c d	**a** b c d	a **b** c d
□	a b c **d**	a b **c** d	a **b** c d	**a** b c d	**a** b c d

	page 107	page 108	page 109	page 110	page 111
○	**a** b c d	**a** b c	a **b** c	**a** b c d	a b c **d**
△	a **b** c d	a **b** c	**a** b c	a b **c** d	a **b** c d
□	a **b** c d	a **b** c	**a** b c	**a** b c d	**a** b c d